W9-AXX-646

LEADING IT

THE TOUGHEST JOB IN THE WORLD

IS SURVIVOR
PUBLISHING

LEADING IT: THE TOUGHEST JOB IN THE WORLD

Published by IS Survivor Publishing, 6272 Sequoia Circle, Eden Prairie, Minnesota 55346, (952) 949-2444.

Visit our Web site at www.issurvivor.com.

First printing 2004

ISBN 978-0-9749354-0-9

LCCN 2004091705

Book/cover design and production by Tim Bitney

What Bob Lewis's readers say

▶ "First, let me say that I read your column every week; for me it is the most valuable part of InfoWorld."

▶ "Your articles are always enlightening."

▶ "I've been cleaning out my study, discovering (literally) years' worth of your Survival Guide columns that I'd torn or cut out of InfoWorld. I've been enjoying reading them again …"

▶ "Each week, I look forward to reading your column in the InfoWorld Magazine. It's the first thing that I turn to, and I often share it with others in my company."

▶ "I enjoy your articles, keep up the great work."

▶ "Thank you, EVER so much, for a very well put first two paragraphs in your InfoWorld 01.07.02 article!"

▶ "Bravo to your write-up on Campfire Wisdom. I was fortunate to be a part of that kind of scenario-based design, and can attest to the fact that it does work!"

▶ "I just read your column. Thank you. I loved it. I look forward to reading each of your columns."

▶ "Your article is oh, so sadly true! I too, having been an IT manager for so many years shook my head often as my own staff would treat my 'customers' like c___. And I agree that they are end-users ... Strategic Planning Consultants (at least the non-IT, non-Bob Lewis types) constantly want to turn everyone into 'customers'".

▶ "Oh, how I love this topic. I have to laugh or I would cry."

▶ "Bob, this is great stuff. If it only happened more often."

▶ "What a great column."

▶ "Just a quick thank you to let you know how much I enjoy your articles in InfoWorld ... Thanks."

▶ "Excellent article! This is one that will be cut out and sent to my manager and brand me as corporate troublemaker!"

▶ "As an avid reader of your column, I just had to respond to this one as it is so right on the money!"

▶ "Your column is about the only thing I'm guaranteed to read when InfoWorld arrives, because you so often summarize a situation succinctly and rationally (two attributes sadly lacking in most of what I read nowadays), not to mention humorously."

WHAT READERS ASK BOB LEWIS:

▶ "I have a problem. Any ideas on what I can do about it?"

▶ "How can I ... ?"

▶ "Any thoughts ...?"

▶ "I'm trying to solve ... can you help?"

▶ "I need advice ..."

▶ "What should I do about ...?"

▶ "I need your help ..."

▶ "What's the best way for me to ...?"

▶ "I'm stuck and need a new perspective."

IT leaders know, if they need practical solutions to the situations they face every day, Bob Lewis is the guy to ask.

Dedication

This book is dedicated to my wife, Sharon Link. There is no way to properly express the extent to which she has helped with this effort, mostly without being aware of having done so.

Her support, her practical knowledge of the subject, and her effortless excellence at leadership as a successful business executive, all have found their way into this book.

Table of contents

Acknowledgements

A book like this doesn't happen in a vacuum. Much as I'd like to think so, this isn't material I thought of all by myself when nobody else was looking.

A lot of people deserve mention.

First of all, beyond all others, I'd like to thank the many people who have reported to me over the years. Some liked the experience better than others; in one way or another all have been my guinea pigs, suffering the consequences of my various misconceptions about leadership while helping me find out what works and what doesn't.

Next are the leaders I've reported to and observed during my career in and out of information technology. I've worked for excellent leaders and awful ones, and I learned a lot about leadership from each, although not the same lessons. I'd name names, but then I'd have to tell you who fit into which categories, which would hardly be fair, and in some cases would not stand the test of this nation's libel laws.

I need to thank the chief information officers and other IT leaders I've had as clients and readers of my weekly column. They've served as a valuable sanity check over the years, helping me understand what works and what just sounds like it ought to work. In particular I need to thank Kelly Williams, who was kind enough to review this effort, and also wrote the foreward, and Larry Robbins, who has provided friendship, guidance and leadership throughout our acquaintance. Both are excellent CIOs, with dramatically different, but equally effective ways of practicing the difficult art of leading IT organizations.

Several practical experts reviewed this book in draft form, helping me understand both where the content had to change, and how to make it as persuasive as possible. Barbara Reindl and Brenda Gumbs, two insightful and talented human resources leaders have been the source of excellent insights into various of the eight tasks of leadership, as well as helping me perfect this book. Their help has been invaluable.

Wess Roberts, Nick Corcodilos, and George Colombo have been good friends and helpful reviewers of much of the material that's made its way into this book. Wess's insights into leadership are legendary – his *Leadership Principles of Attila the Hun* remains a classic of which I'll be eternally jealous. Nick, author of *Ask the Headhunter*, the definitive work on hiring and getting hired, is the original source of many of "my" insights into this subject. And George, author of *Killer Customer Care*, has helped me consume a variety of conversational lubricants while deepening my understanding of persuasion and how to help move an organization in your chosen direction.

Steve Nazian, my consulting partner and friend of more decades than either of us would care to admit, did yeoman's duty as copy and content editor, spotting numerous glitches, questionable turns of phrase, and poorly chosen examples for which his suggested alternatives generally proved superior.

Tim Bitney, my partner and friend, is responsible for turning my words into a finished product put together in a form that's readable and, just as important, shippable. Without his efforts and many helpful suggestions, this book wouldn't exist except as a collection of unread Microsoft Word files.

Finally, there's family. My father, Herschell Gordon Lewis, is the acknowledged master of writing persuasively; none of my writing would be more than pedestrian had it not been for his *The Art of Writing Copy*.

My daughters, Kimberly and Erin, didn't really help at all, but that's okay: They've put up with their father's strange hobby while helping me understand that whatever minor degree of celebrity it's provided over the years really doesn't mean very much in the greater scheme of things. For their love, support, and exceedingly strange senses of humor, I'm continually grateful.

So if you don't like the book, by all means, blame all of these people! *It's their fault!* But if you like it, I'll be happy to take the credit.

Foreword

By Kelly Williams

Chief Information Officer

I met Bob Lewis about two and a half years ago, shortly after I had agreed to become the chief information officer of a national mortgage lender. I had walked into some pretty hefty challenges in the form of a company that had managed to do just about everything wrong with regard to information technology. I was hip-deep in a real mess and I needed some help, so I called a fellow who advertised the ability to do an "Information Technology Assessment." When Bob agreed to work with us, my expectations were pretty modest. I thought I'd see a pro forma effort that would document our most obvious problems, supplemented with some canned advice. In other words, I was expecting a typical IT management consulting engagement. What I received was the experience of working with a refreshingly honest and intelligent individual who provided me with an unexpectedly large measure of insight, wisdom, and – because it is Bob, after all – unabashed opinions.

With the publication of this book, I will now have the luxury of being able to tap into Bob's wit and wisdom on the topic of leadership without rummaging through my notes from our many conversations – a single point of reference that captures many of his thoughts and much of his advice. Whether you are a brand-new CIO (or are thinking about the day when you will become one), or someone who has taken more than one stroll around the IT management track, you will undoubtedly find something of value within these covers.

A word of warning: Bob's writing style is a unique blend of common sense, academic expertise, and humor. With it, and unlike many of his contemporaries who apparently believe that obfuscation builds character, he manages to turn fairly complex topics into very easy to read and understand essays. Don't be fooled. Even though you might actually enjoy yourself while reading this book, I assure you that you will also be learning something valuable about the dynamics of leadership, about your organizations and about yourselves.

What is leadership anyhow?

If the definition is wrong, so is the rest of it

A mystique has accreted around the simple term "leadership" as if it were something ineffable – an aura that surrounds certain individuals, conferring upon them numinous powers beyond human understanding, but nonetheless vital for the conduct of human affairs.

In an attempt to penetrate the mists surrounding the subject, various experts have conducted studies and published numerous progress reports. I imagine them as a flock of urban anthropologists, following "leaders" around, living among them, recording their activities and distilling their essence.

Now, I do not wish to ridicule these hardy souls, for among their writings are valuable insights. In many cases, though, they have committed one of two complementary sins: They've either distorted the concept of leadership by making it one dimensional, or they've over complicated it.

This book deals with the leadership of information technology organizations … if not the toughest job in the world, definitely one of the tougher. It attempts to summarize what I've read about the subject, observed first-hand, and on occasion practiced or experienced myself. I wrote it because in my consulting business I've worked with quite a few talented individuals who, when promoted to leadership positions, hadn't the slightest idea what it meant to change from being an individual contributor to leading individual contributors, let alone leading other leaders. Worse, since they were promoted due to their accomplishments as individual contributors they had no particular reason to think being a leader was anything beyond being a top-notch individual contributor only more so.

> *"Management is doing things right— Leadership is doing the right things."*
>
> **– Peter Drucker & Walter Bemis**

Or, having decided they did need a different set of skills, they then "chose a guru" and attempted to learn how to lead as they might learn to bake a cake – by following a recipe. Inevitably the results were disappointing, because while one batch of flour, sugar, eggs and butter all behave the same way as the next, each batch of people has unique characteristics and dynamics. You can't lead people through the simple formulas you find in management cookbooks.

Which doesn't mean leadership is an intellectually demanding discipline. Quite the contrary: Leadership is tough the way digging a ditch is tough, not the way tensor calculus is tough. Done right it's demanding work that requires ...

But I'm getting ahead of myself. Before we can decide what makes someone a successful leader we have to agree on a definition. And there's no shortage of definitions from which to choose.

Those well-known philosophers of business, Peter Drucker and Walter Bemis, for example, define leadership as doing the right things, as opposed to management which means getting things done. Admiral Grace Hopper sailed around the problem of definition through the use of examples, pointing out that "you manage things, you lead people".

While both are valuable thoughts, neither succeeds in defining the term, I'm afraid. Many highly effective leaders have chosen execrable goals (Hitler and Stalin spring to mind); many admirable human beings, who have chosen worthwhile goals as well, have failed to lead people to achieve them. You need seek no further than Jimmy Carter's tenure as president of the United States to find an example of this. Clearly, leadership is both more and less than doing the right things.

> *"You manage things, you lead people."*
>
> — **Admiral Grace Hopper**

Nor is Admiral Hopper's approach more successful: Things, after all, don't manage themselves – people are involved in the process, and the day-to-day grind of managing things inevitably involves more prosaic interactions with those individuals than those involved in leadership.

The definition of leadership is actually quite obvious and requires no subtlety: *You lead when others follow.* Leadership is neither more nor less than getting other people to go where you want them to go. If you make them believe it was their idea in the first place, so much the better.

That's tough enough. If you want to be an admirable leader, there's even more involved.

None of it, however, is particularly complicated, which is why great intellect is more often possessed by the powers who sit behind thrones than by those who inhabit them. While true idiots rarely succeed in leadership roles, it's equally rare for geniuses to do so. Leaders require clarity far more than they require deep understanding, courage far more than scholarship, and consistency more than calculus.

Leaders manage relationships in four directions: North, which is to say with those to whom they report; East, to their peers, who they can only influence; West, to those who make use of the products and services their organizations produce; and South, to those reporting to them. Being adept at all four of these is a challenge for any leader. For an IT leader it's even tougher.

> *"If people are following you're leading. Otherwise you aren't."*
> — Bob Lewis

IT is a complex discipline. If it isn't rocket science it's awfully close. When you lead IT, you lead programmers, analysts, database analysts, enterprise architects and the rest of the cast and crew required to keep a company's systems running and to extend them as necessary. These are very bright people, often narrowly focused, with diverse interests and a high degree of independence. Many are constitutionally incapable of respecting leaders who can't deal with them on their terms.

That's South. The other three relationship dimensions are rarely willing to acknowledge the complexity of the discipline, let alone learn anything about it themselves. Instead, they insist that the IT leader keep things simple.

Balancing the demands and issues of these four relationship directions is what makes leading IT organizations a particularly difficult challenge.

This book is about leadership. Its focus is IT leadership, but for the most part the principles it presents will be just as useful in any leadership role.

The book provides a job description for leadership, boiling it down to eight basic tasks. Four are concrete, tangible and direct. The remainder are softer, qualitative and subjective.

The four concrete tasks are:
▸ Envisioning the future
▸ Delegating
▸ Making decisions
▸ Staffing

The four remaining softer tasks are:
▸ Motivating employees (and everyone else)
▸ Building and maintaining teams
▸ Establishing culture
▸ Communicating

If you master the eight tasks of leadership you'll become a more effective leader. Whether you become a better leader is up to you, "better" being a purely subjective, somewhat ethical evaluation. You're responsible for your ethical choices; far be it from me to superimpose my values on you.

How effective you are is something everyone can agree on. Either others are following you or they aren't. That isn't hard to determine, only hard to achieve.

So welcome to the wonderful world of IT leadership. It's the toughest job in the world. And if it isn't, it's certainly tough enough.

CHAPTER ONE

Envisioning the future

*There's little more ridiculous than a leader shouting,
"Follow me!" and when the troops ask, "Where to?"
the leader responds, "I don't know!"*

Of all the management clichés, "vision" might just be the most annoying. Admit it: Whenever you hear someone say, "Here's my vision," you sit back, sigh, and say to yourself, "Here we go again – more talk, no action, and no real ideas, either. Beam me up, Scotty!"

Or as Ainsley Throckmorton put it when he became president of Bangor Seminary in Maine, "First management had plans, and then strategic plans. Now we have vision, and we're only one small step from hallucination."

Ever since President George Bush Sr. had trouble with the "vision thing," vision has fallen into disrepute. That's the trouble with clichés. Through triteness and misuse they discredit valuable concepts. And when it comes to the leadership job description, everything starts with the ability to envision and describe a compelling future.

Leadership is, in fact, purely about the future. If the job is defined as getting other people to go where you want them to go, then the logical first step is deciding where you want them to go. There's little more ridiculous than a leader shouting, "Follow me!" and when the troops ask, "Where to?" the leader responds, "I don't know!"

Talk about ways to inspire confidence.

Leadership is about creating the future instead of waiting for it to happen. Which is to say, it's about driving change. With only one exception, if there's no change there's no leadership.

The exception? Sometimes leaders are required to resist an undesirable change. In geopolitics it might be an invading army, in business a new competitor invading your traditional markets.

And this exception validates the rule[1], because ignoring a threat rarely makes it go away. The act of resisting undesired change calls for envisioning a different kind of change, not for envisioning business as usual. Franklin Delano Roosevelt was a great leader, not because he ignored the Great Depression, the Nazi threat in Europe and the sneak attack at Pearl Harbor, but because he responded to each of these threats, envisioning new paths for this country and persuading its citizens to follow those paths.

What constitutes vision, and how is it different from the dreaded "Mission Statement"? Or do you need both to lead an organization? And what's a charter, and how does it differ from the other two?

Here's one way of looking at it that might help you: A vision is about a new way to be, a mission is something to be accomplished. John F. Kennedy's famous commitment to put a man on the moon described a mission. To illustrate the distinction, someday we'll have a president who envisions a future in which space travel is commonplace, integrated into our society and economy. That truly would be a compelling vision.

Also noteworthy: For project teams, the mission describes

[1] As Ambrose Bierce pointed out, the idea that exceptions prove the rule is bogus, the result of a mis-translation. The original Latin is *"Exceptio probat regulam."* Exceptions *probe* the rule ... that is, they test it, which makes all kinds of sense.

completion; the vision provides context. For operational organizations, the mission describes the present and is largely a tool for managing, whereas the vision, which describes the future, is where leadership begins.

And: Vision is the beginning of strategy. Vision paints a compelling account of a future that's different from the present in one or more fundamental ways; strategy includes a plan for achieving that future.

What's a charter? It's a document that fleshes out a mission, discussing context, scope, goals, deliverables, resources, and governance. It's a management tool, not a leadership tool, which is to say it's far more closely linked to actual work. Just as strategy fleshes out vision, so charters flesh out missions.

Visions and missions have a few things in common:

▶ They're both brief and to the point – simple declarative sentences that leave no doubt as to their meaning. Jack Welch's well-known vision for General Electric – that it will only be in businesses that can be first or second in their markets – is hard to misunderstand. (An easy test: If it has a list of bullets, more than two sentences, or qualifiers, it is neither a vision nor a mission. Instead you'll be well on your way to writing a contract. In particular, if it includes the word "by" followed by an explanation of how you're going to go about the task … eliminate the word "by" and everything that follows it.)

▶ The meaning, not the phrasing, is what's important. You aren't crafting the Pledge of Allegiance. You're communicating a common understanding as to what your organization is trying to accomplish. Spend your energy on the idea, not on word-smithery. Once you fully understand what you're trying to do, you'll find the phrasing is easy.

▶ They're prescriptive, not descriptive. Put differently, they're useful in making choices. A vision or mission that validates everything you currently do or might wish to do is neither mission nor vision. It's just an excuse.

▶ They're specific. It isn't information unless it helps make a choice. Compare a vague generality like, "We'll exceed our customers' expectations," with Jack Welch's requirement that GE will only be in businesses that can be first or second in their markets and you'll understand the difference.

So. How does a great leader go about arriving at a vision?

Historically, some have wandered into the wilderness for awhile, chewing on peyote buttons, fasting for a few weeks, letting poisonous snakes bite them, or otherwise inducing the hallucinations Ainsley Throckmorton described.

I don't recommend it, but if it works for you, go for it, especially if you're smart enough to choose the best path by yourself, and are a sufficiently charismatic orator that you can persuade everyone in your organization to follow you, just because you've chosen it and it's a good idea.

Good luck.

Another popular but sub-optimal way to arrive at a vision is pure consensus. Bring everyone, or at least everyone who reports to you into a room and encourage them to present their views. Your role is to facilitate the discussion until either a consensus emerges or everyone gets tired and pretends to agree so they can get to the cocktails and *hors d'oeuvres*. We'll explore consensus decision-making in more detail later on. For now, ask yourself how it is you're leading when you leave choosing a vision to a group process in which your role is relegated to simple facilitation. The group will understand that *you aren't leading,* merely facilitating.

The best way I know of to develop a vision looks pretty

similar, though. The only difference is your role in the discussion, which is to shape it, direct it, and at key points either force or make decisions, in the end presenting the result as *your* vision – both yours and more than yours, inviting each individual in the organization to adopt as his or her own.

It's a tough balancing act. For a vision to be effective you need to build a consensus around it. But to lead *your* organization it must be your vision. First-rate leaders are able to achieve this balance. Acceptable leaders arrive at a vision some other way, but do arrive at a vision.

The rest? They don't really lead, because they're sitting still. How can anyone follow someone who isn't moving?

So ask yourself, your team, and anyone else whose opinion you value: What should the future look like, and what's your organization's role in making it look like that? Then distill their ideas, internalize them, and shape them into a coherent perspective. To be most effective, do this in open, working sessions in which you do more than simply facilitate, but less than simply decide on your own.

Once you can articulate the future, in just a couple of short sentences, you're ready to lead other people...in other words, your organization...to get there.

SUMMARY

▶ Leadership is about creating the future. People can't follow you if you don't know where you want to go, or what you want to build, or what you want to accomplish.

▶ Even the act of resisting a change requires the definition of a different change. You can't lead by standing still.

▶ Vision statements describe a new and compelling way to be. Mission statements are something to be accomplished. Both should be concise, simple statements. Five or fewer words is best.

▶ Vision and mission are prescriptive and specific, not descriptive; certainly they are not vague. They drive choices.

▶ Meaning matters. Phrasing doesn't.

CHAPTER TWO

Delegation

*Leaders delegate. The best leaders delegate goals
rather than tasks or activities.*

Vagueness is the enemy of leadership. Vagueness is the enemy of communication.

Therefore, leadership is communication.

No, not really, although communication is one of the most important tools at a leader's disposal *(Chapter 8)*. The problem with communication is that you need something significant to communicate.

Like, for example, what people should be working on, and why it's important for them to do so.

When you boil it all down, there are just two ways to tell people what to do. You can either tell them to do something, or you can tell them to accomplish something. You can, in other words, focus your own attention on either activities or results.

Which you prefer has a lot to do with whether you think about the world as a manager or a leader. At the risk of undue repetition, leadership happens when people follow you – when they go where you want them to go under their own steam. When you focus on results they have to go there under their own power. When you focus on activities you pull them along.

That's just one of the disadvantages of focusing on

activities: It makes you work too hard. There are others, like its de-motivating impact on those being dragged and the risk that just maybe you don't always know the best way to accomplish a task.

To be fair, there are situations in which you do have to direct activities. The distinction between leadership and management isn't that one is good and the other bad. Problems arise when you fail to strike the proper balance, managing when you should be leading or vice versa.

Leadership isn't about telling people how to do their jobs. It's about defining the results the organization needs and leaving it to others to figure out the best way to get it done.

In a word, it's about delegation.

HOW TO HAVE DISCUSSIONS

"Discuss" doesn't mean "direct." When you discuss something with a staff member you listen and ask questions far more than you talk and explain answers – you help him or her succeed. When you direct – when you talk and explain, allowing the staff member to listen and ask questions – you're trying to prevent failure, a far different matter.

These aren't alternatives so much as they are the opposite ends of a continuum. As a generality, conversations about goals will have more direction and less discussion; conversations about methods will be the reverse. In both cases you're best off avoiding the extremes: In conversations about goals, pure direction makes you appear closed-minded; in conversations about methods, pure discussion means you aren't sharing your knowledge of the subject.

Most managers learn the skill of delegation early in their transition from being an individual contributor to leading others. They learn to delegate tasks. To delegate a task you:

▶ Define the deliverable, scope of the effort, its business context, the resources you can make available, and the level of authority you're going to delegate.

▶ Decide who among your staff is best-suited to the task.

▶ Discuss the task with the individual you choose and the means for undertaking it. (Be prepared to adjust some of the decisions you made prior to the meeting, too.)

▶ Meet on a regular basis to review progress, explore issues, clarify ambiguities, and otherwise ensure the task remains on track.

▶ Review the deliverable at the end, request and review final changes, and either accept or reject the result.

▶ Monitor the implementation.

One other note: Some tasks create a deliverable and finish – they're projects. Others create deliverables on an on-going basis – they're *operations*. The rules are pretty much the same regardless, and task delegation is an important management skill. It's relation to leadership, though, is limited.

Leaders delegate strategic goals, and in doing so make the future happen.

The mechanics of delegating a strategic goal are similar to those for delegating a task. The main difference is that where task delegation results in a specific, tangible deliverable or product, when you delegate a strategic goal the best you can do is measure progress against it, and even then it can be awfully hard to determine whether progress is the result of the actions taken, or for that matter whether lack of progress

LEADERSHIP INSIGHT: PROCESSES VS PRACTICES

Don't blame Deming. He created the discipline of statistical process control for factories, never imagining that an army of unimaginative consultants would later force-fit every activity in the universe into the process paradigm, whether or not it belonged there.

Not all activities are processes – well-defined and documented sequences of actions that lead to repeatable, predictable results. By definition it's only a process when it's repeated, which means it's only a process when you need to create the same result over and over. That's what factories are for, whether they're physical manufacturing facilities, insurance forms processing departments, or computer operations centers.

Other activities are practices – professional disciplines. Where processes strive to create repeatable, predictable results and do so, in part, by moving intelligence from individual experts into the process itself, practices strive to create unique predictable results. They deal with similar but distinct situations – lawsuits, projects, or the marketing of a company's products. But every lawsuit, project or marketing campaign is different, so their conduct requires expert practitioners.

Cooking is a process, which is why cookbooks work. Haute cuisine, in contrast, is a practice. There's no cookbook for creating new and tasty victuals – no sequence of steps that leads to a new and wonderful recipe every time.

Considered in these terms, Leadership itself is a practice, not a process, and concerns itself more with practices than processes.

indicates inappropriate action, or just that not enough time has passed.

But we're getting ahead of ourselves. The term "strategic" is easy to bandy about, but harder to pin down, and in these benighted days of bureaucratic doubletalk it's often used as a synonym for "important" – a worthless way of looking at things.

As we're using the term, at least, you're dealing with strategy when the goals change. Strategy isn't about achieving a future that's just like the present, only better. Those are tactical goals – they're about operational improvement. One way to tell the difference: achievement of tactical goals improves an organization's key measures. Achievement of strategic goals changes an organization's key measures.

Here's how leaders make the future happen: They determine what strategic changes are needed to transform the organization from its current state into its desired future state – an intellectually challenging process that requires persistence, a high level of coordination, and significant investment in time, money, and resources – and then delegate responsibility for those changes.

So when the leader of an organization delegates strategic goals it means he or she has envisioned some desirable future state, determined what specific changes have to happen in order to achieve it, and articulated each of these specific changes as a goal. He or she then delegates these goals while still maintaining personal ownership of all of them.

Many CEOs try to make do by asking everyone to behave in ways consistent with their envisioned future, figuring that if everyone does so the company will achieve the desired future state. Occasionally that can even work. Usually, it results in unfocused activities that lead to disappointing results. Why? It's hard to build something when you don't have a design to

THE "NEED TO KNOW" APPROACH

Some leaders like to work on a "need to know" basis. They give specific instructions to each direct report and keep the overall goal to themselves.

This can work for you too, but only if you're very lucky. If the greatest risk to your strategy is having your competitors discover it prematurely, you might have to work this way. Otherwise, it's a bad idea.

To illustrate, imagine you have to get five carloads of passengers to a particular destination. You have several choices. You can:

▶ "Ride caravan" with your car in the lead and the others following you like beads on a string.

▶ Provide specific driving directions to each driver.

▶ Give every driver the destination address so they can figure out how to get there independently.

It seems pretty clear that doing all three maximizes your chance for success. Riding caravan means everyone can follow you to the destination; driving directions allow them to get there if you get separated; the destination address allows drivers to recover from wrong turns and also allows those who know a better route than you do get there easier and faster.

Which means that in business you maximize your chances for success by making sure everyone understands the vision, understands their role in helping achieve it, understands your thoughts on how they can help you achieve it, but doesn't feel constrained to only do things your way in helping the company get there.

work from. Leaders who take this approach haven't delegated strategic goals – in effect, they delegate the strategy itself, and in a way that disconnects it from their vision and precludes coherent action. Don't do this.

The technique for delegating goals is similar to what's needed when delegating tasks, but different in a number of respects. First of all, it's best accomplished through meetings with your direct reports, not alone. Here are the steps:

▶ Determine what the goals ... the strategic changes ... must be to achieve the envisioned future.

▶ Cast each goal in terms that are as concrete as possible.

▶ Construct measures to determine progress toward each goal. Don't worry if many of the measures are subjective – that's inevitable when dealing with strategic goals. Do, however, worry about formulating each measure so that it behaves properly, improving only when the company makes real progress toward the goal.

▶ Determine who should lead in the achievement of each of the goals.

▶ Meet on a regular basis to review progress, discuss issues, clarify ambiguities, and otherwise ensure the task remains on track.

▶ Review the deliverable at the end, request and review final changes, and either accept or reject the result.

▶ Don't stop paying attention once the change has been achieved. While formally speaking, the ongoing monitoring of results falls more into the category of management than leadership, leaders who ignore the value of day-to-day hard work can find themselves lacking in dedicated followers.

Delegation requires one of the most difficult psychological

changes people undergo as they shift their perspective from being individual contributors to being leaders. It happens in stages.

An individual contributor promoted to front-line supervision typically knows how to do the job very well – often that's why he was promoted in the first place. Since he knows how to do the job so well, he supervises by being just as sure as he can be that the employees he supervises *follow the process*. In other words, he makes sure they do it *his* way.

That isn't necessarily a bad thing, either. In manufacturing, where your goal is to create a succession of identical items at a predictable cost and schedule, and quality is defined as adherence to specifications, you need employees to follow a well-defined repeatable process.

You need them to be on a constant lookout for ways to improve the process, too, but process improvement isn't the same thing as improvisation. Of necessity, supervisors in manufacturing situations must oversee activity, and have relatively little opportunity to delegate. As a result, their opportunity to practice delegation is constrained.

Those who supervise non-manufacturing situations have a different set of challenges. By definition they don't manage processes in the first place, so they have more freedom to give their employees more freedom.

A front-line manager in this situation – perhaps running a small department – is already accustomed to having more independence of action. An individual with this background often will be less comfortable enforcing procedures than a manufacturing supervisor, and also might experience some difficulty with the transition from being a superior individual contributor, whom peers consult about difficult issues, to a manager, kept out of the loop by staff until the difficult issue has been resolved.

FOLLOWERSHIP

Imagine, if you will, an organization that's chock full o' leaders. What comes to mind? Too many chefs in the kitchen, that's what. As the great science fiction writer E. E. "Doc" Smith's characters used to say in his epic *Lensman* series, "We can't all play first chair violin. Some of us have to push air through the tuba."

We do. Which calls for a special, highly prized trait called "followership." Followership means accepting the direction set by a leader – following – but in such a way that you make it your own, providing leadership within your own domain that advances the whole organization in its intended direction.

Leaders can only delegate goals when the leaders reporting to them are capable of followership. If you want to be thought of as a leader, it's a skill you'll develop above all others. Its ultimate value to you is higher than you might think: As you increase your followership abilities, you also increase your understanding of what you're asking of those reporting to you.

Without followership, an abundance of leadership will result in an organization that tears itself apart. With followership, an organization can achieve whatever goals it sets for itself.

SUMMARY

▶ Leadership is delegation: If you want people to follow your lead, they need to know what they're supposed to do.

▶ Leaders can either delegate tasks or goals. Both are necessary, depending on the circumstances and the employee. The latter has much more power.

▶ To delegate a task:

▷ Define the deliverable, scope of the effort, its business context, the resources you can make available, and the level of authority you're going to delegate.

▷ Decide who among your staff is best-suited to the task.

▷ Discuss the task with the individual you choose and the means for undertaking it. (Be prepared to adjust some of the decisions you made prior to the meeting, too.)

▷ Meet on a regular basis to review progress, explore issues, clarify ambiguities, and otherwise ensure the task remains on track.

▷ Review the deliverable at the end, request and review final changes, and either accept or reject the result.

▷ Monitor the implementation.

▶ To delegate a goal:

▷ Determine what the goals ... the strategic changes ... must be to achieve the envisioned future.

▷ Cast each goal in terms that are as concrete as possible.

▷ Construct measures to determine progress toward each goal. Don't worry if many of the measures are subjective – that's inevitable when dealing with strategic goals. Do, however, worry about formulating each measure so that it behaves properly, improving only when the company makes progress.

▷ Determine who should lead in the achievement of each of the goals.

▷ Meet on a regular basis to review progress, discuss issues, clarify ambiguities, and otherwise ensure the task remains on track.

▷ Review the deliverable at the end, request and review final changes, and either accept or reject the result.

▷ Monitor the implementation

▶ The ultimate goal of delegation is to establish followership: Accepting the direction set by a leader – following – but in such a way that you make it your own, providing leadership within your own domain that advances the whole organization in its intended direction. Leaders can only delegate goals when the leaders reporting to them are capable of followership, so in a very real sense, your ability to foster it is the limiting factor in your ability to lead.

CHAPTER THREE

Making decisions

Decisions commit or deny time, money, and staff.
Everything else is just talking about it.

In the final analysis, leadership is about decisions.

Vision and mission establish the subject matter. Delegation assigns responsibility and authority. Communication explains the results. And so on. Every other leadership responsibility is either preamble or follow-on to the core responsibility: To decide.

You'd think leaders would focus more attention on doing it well, wouldn't you?

Yet many don't even know what a decision actually is, and many who do treat decisions the way you or I might treat an acquaintance with a highly visible and unpleasant-looking skin condition – that is, they try their best to avoid getting anywhere near them.

My dictionary defines "decide"[2] as "to determine or settle (a question, controversy, struggle, etc.) by giving victory to one side." As is true of so many dictionary definitions, this one is simultaneously completely true and quite unhelpful. Sure, when you make a decision you choose among the possible alternatives, but that misses the essence of the beast.

---

[2] In the usual, helpful fashion of a dictionary, "decision" is defined as what you get when you decide.

Here's the critical point: If it doesn't either commit or deny time, money, and staff, it isn't a decision.

It's just talking.

To put it in slightly different terms, if it doesn't lead to action, what's the point? And in business, action requires the commitment of time, money and staff.

No? How about this: How can you determine whether you have the authority to make a decision in your organization? You can if it requires no staff other than those reporting to you, if it requires no funding beyond those you control in your budget, and requires nobody's time other than your own and that of those reporting to you.

These are the factors that determine the boundaries of your authority. They define, in other words, which decisions are yours and which ones aren't.

DECISION-MAKING PROCESSES

When you first enter the ranks of management there's a certain headiness to it. Before, all you could do was recommend. Now you can decide.

As a result, many inexperienced managers start deciding stuff. Where other leaders lose the paperwork or go through elaborate, delay-inducing processes so as to play it safe, I'm going to be decisive and get it done!

Many new managers, in other words, have a tendency to rely on an authoritarian, command-and-control style of decision-making.

Unfortunately, the synonym for command-and-control is "fast-and-stupid." It just isn't the best way to go about things.

A different breed of novice manager overdoes the polar opposite of authoritarian decision-making, over-relying on consensus-building. Where authoritarian decisions are fast and stupid, consensus processes are, by their nature, slow, and often result in unattractive compromises whose only virtue is satisfying everyone enough that they get on board.

It isn't that authoritarian and consensus decision-making are bad. It's that managers who use only one style of decision-making are like musicians who play on one-string violins. In theory they can still play all the notes, but they'll never play as well as someone who commands the whole instrument.

Managers have five different processes at their disposal for making decisions. None is good or bad in any absolute sense. Each is suited to a different set of circumstances. The trick is knowing which one to use in a particular situation.[3]

The five are:

▶ Authoritarianism

▶ Consensus

▶ Consultation

▶ Delegation

▶ Democracy

If you don't have time to read the whole chapter, Table 3.1 summarizes and compares these methods of making a decision.

TABLE 3.1/ *DECISION PROCESS SUMMARY*

Decision process	Speed	Buy-in	Cost	Quality
Authoritarianism	High	Low	Low	Low
Consensus	Low	High	High	Medium
Consultation	Medium	Med./High	Medium	High
Delegation	Varies	Med./Low	Varies	High[4]
Democracy	Low	Medium	Medium	Low

[3] Yes, you're deciding which one to use. As you'll see, even this decision has implications for staffing and time, although it rarely has a direct impact on your budget.

[4] But risky, depending on the decision, who you delegated it to, and the decision process decided upon by the delegatee.

AUTHORITARIANISM

You have a decision to make. It's your decision to make – that is, it's within your domain of responsibility and authority.

So you make it. What's the problem?

Sometimes, there is no problem. When the most important factors are speed and decisiveness – which is to say, when it's a crisis – make an authoritarian decision and make it stick. In a crisis, even a bad decision is better than no decision. People who are waiting for a decision mill around doing nothing.

Meanwhile, the enemy is on the move, or the walls that

TRUST YOUR GUT?

And now, a word about relying on your gut feelings.

In Star Wars, Luke Skywalker could trust his feelings because the Force took care of the nasty details. Unless the Force is with you, the hard work known as "thinking" should be your dominant method of decision-making.

Think of your gut feeling as a quick-and-dirty way to apply your experience (good news) and biases (bad news) to the decision at hand. In an emergency, trusting your gut is far better than panicking. When you aren't in an emergency, and have time for reflection, the only role your gut should play is to warn you that you might have missed something important.

And even then, don't trust it. Fear of a decision – or the flip side of this coin, falling in love with a particular course of action – will cause your gut to give you unreliable advice.

When the time comes to make a decision, use your brain if you have the time. That's what it's there for.

were weakened by the earthquake are starting to crumble, or the person you love is a block away from you, ticked off, and moving fast.

Do something – anything! – before it's too late.

Whatever you decide to do probably won't be the best course of action, but at least you'll be doing something, and in a crisis that's always better than sitting on your hands.

CONSENSUS

In a consensus decision, not everyone has to agree with it, but everyone has to agree to it. It might not be how I'd do it, but I can live with this, and so can everyone else who participated in the consensus process.

Where authoritarian decisions are fast (and cheap) but rarely lead to the most desirable course of action, consensus decisions are slow and expensive. Worse, they rarely lead to the best decisions either. Because they have to satisfy everyone, they're usually messy.

Why would you put yourself through a process that's time-consuming and expensive and rarely leads to the best result?

Answer: When you have to, of course. The advantage to a consensus is that everyone's name is on it and everyone is committed. Nobody gets to second-guess it later. In a word, you get buy-in.

Sometimes, that's important even when you could make the decision yourself. Smart CEOs charting a new business strategy create at least the illusion of consensus among their executive team, for example, because mere acquiescence isn't enough for success. Everyone on the team needs to display "followership"[5] which means they need to embrace the strategy as their own.

---

[5] See Chapter Two – Delegation – for more on this subject.

LEADERSHIP IS EASIEST IN A CRISIS

Crisis provides motivation and mutual trust, something leaders have to provide themselves in less urgent times. Crisis also provides alignment of purpose, allowing leaders the luxury of authoritarian decision-making.

In less urgent times, leaders must consult with others, achieving alignment of purpose through the hard, delicate, necessary work of careful consensus building.

Leading an organization is much, much harder when there's no emergency. Consider Franklin Delano Roosevelt: His greatness resulted less from his resolve following the attack on Pearl Harbor than from his response to the Great Depression. By putting people back to work and through his weekly radio broadcasts he gave people hope. Arguably, it was by restoring America's belief in its ability to solve its problems that he could lead the country through World War II.

Leadership is easiest in a crisis, which is why so many bad leaders create crises when none exist. This is as true when a bad manager uses preposterous deadlines to justify a project death march as when a corrupt dictator distracts citizens from his own repressive policies by starting a war.

Crises only last so long. Then the situation becomes business as usual, and the crisis, in the eyes of those you lead, is over. What's left is all the hard work. That's when your mettle as a leader will really be tested.

And then there are situations in which nobody has the authority to make a decision. Sometimes a group of peers agrees that something needs to be done. How can they decide on a course of action?

It has to be a consensus (or a vote, which we'll get to later on ... but let's hope it doesn't come down to that!)

Some leaders use consensus decision-making as a hedge against failure – as a way to spread the blame. This can be politically astute, but it's a bad habit to get into because it's a tempting way to avoid taking responsibility for decisions that are yours to make.

The trickiest aspect to consensus decision-making is ensuring you really have a consensus, which means everyone has committed to the decision and not just acquiesced during the meeting with varying degrees of sincerity. There's a fine but very definite line separating honesty ("It isn't how I would have done it but it's a good plan and I'm committed to it,") from undercutting ("I finally gave up – I'm going along with it, but I don't really think it's going to work.")

The specific techniques for dealing with the latter are beyond the scope of this book. Suffice it to say they're yet another factor that makes consensus decision-making so expensive.

To be proficient at leadership you must be able to drive a group to consensus and hold its members to it afterward. Excellence at leadership requires you to be very selective in choosing when to do so.

CONSULTATION

Consultative decision-making – the process of gathering everyone's opinion while reserving the decision for yourself – is the mainstay of effective leadership. It strikes a comfortable balance between speed, cost, and buy-in while

THE OODA LOOP

Developed by Colonel John Boyd during the Korean War, OODA, which stands for Observation, Orientation, Decision, Action, describes a process for defeating opponents in contests ranging from simple games to theatre-scale military maneuvering.

Here a quick summary: Observation means gathering information. Consultative decision-making requires this as part of its definition; it's also intrinsic to any good consensus, and it's quite helpful in a democracy, assuming you value informed voters.

Orientation includes understanding of yourself and your biases, and how you synthesize observations into your process for making Decisions. Your take-home lesson? While no human being is ever truly unbiased, smart leaders achieve the next-best thing: They know their biases so they aren't imprisoned by them. Put it differently, orientation is the difference between using information to guide actions and searching for ammunition – selectively gathering information to justify a decision already made, which is what most people do instead of truly gathering information.

The last letter of OODA stands for Action ... otherwise what's the point of a decision? ... which in turn leads to new Observations, completing the loop.

This is a grossly oversimplified treatment of a fascinating and important subject. When you've finished this book, spend some time researching it. You'll find it time well spent.[6]

[6] Thanks to Curt Sahakian of the Corporate Partnering Institute for introducing it to me.

maximizing the quality of the final decision – so long as you're qualified to make it, of course. If you aren't, you should delegate the decision to someone who is.

There isn't a lot more to be said about consultative decision-making, other than this: When you consult someone about a decision you've asked for their help. Phrase your request this way, be open to their ideas, and take them into account when you make your final decision, even if you ultimately choose a different course of action.

Finally, remember that you owe everyone you've consulted an explanation and accounting of your decision. You'll have taken some advice while not incorporating other ideas into it. That's as it should be.

The key to success is making clear the difference between valuing someone's advice and following it. If anyone has a hard time accepting this, your response is that a decision requires you to choose among alternatives, and ideas that are well-suited to one alternative might not fit a different one at all.

DELEGATION

We just spent an entire chapter on the subject of delegation, and here it is again. One of the responsibilities you can delegate is a decision. Another is a recommendation. So long as you make it clear which of the two you're delegating, it's fine.

Just remember: Always delegate a decision when the person you're delegating the decision to has more expertise in the subject than you do; never delegate a decision when you aren't willing to live with the risk of a bad one, and remember: Delegation isn't of itself a way to make a decision. The person to whom you delegate a decision must first choose how to make it, through either an authoritarian, consensus, or consultative process.

DEMOCRACY

Last, and most definitely least, is democracy. It's been described as the worst form of government, except for all the others.

Voting is how a group of peers makes a decision when it either can't reach a consensus or lacks the time and will to try. While not as expensive and time-consuming as consensus decision-making, voting doesn't generate consensus's shared commitment, either. Nor does it generates the quality of consultative decision-making. In a sense, it's the flip side of the authoritarian coin, with the tyranny of the majority replacing the tyranny of the individual decision-maker.

Business isn't a matter of representative government. Use voting as the fall-back to consensus when nobody has the authority to make a decision, and for nothing else.

LAST WORD

Making a decision isn't always the prudent thing to do. Every decision carries with it the risk of events proving you wrong in the future. If your goal is career advancement you might find yourself better off leaving decisions to others. In many organizations, the rewards for making good decisions are few while the penalties for being wrong are harsh. Under these circumstances, promotions come to those who leave the deciding to others, because those others fall by the wayside as they're "held accountable" for their mistakes.

Healthy organizations recognize that not all failure is the result of incompetence. They recognize and reward leadership. If you want to be a successful leader, make sure you work for one of these. Then, as a leader, make sure decisions get made.

It's your job.

SUMMARY

▶ As a leader you have five ways you can make a decision:
    ▷ Authoritarianism
    ▷ Consensus
    ▷ Consultation
    ▷ Delegation
    ▷ Democracy

▶ Each has its place. None is universally appropriate. Effective leaders use all of them, choosing the one best-suited to the circumstances. Ineffective leaders have just one way to make decisions.

▶ See Table 3.1 for details.

CHAPTER FOUR

Staffing

Hire people, not résumés.

If leadership is about getting others to follow – to accomplish your goals through the actions of others – then the importance of selecting the right "others" through which to accomplish your goals is hard to overstate.

Most experienced leaders understand how important it is to select, retain, train, groom and promote the right people.

Inexperienced and ineffective leaders consider staffing a distraction. Perhaps it's the overworked distinction between management and leadership that's to blame: If your focus is on getting things done, it's generally easier to perform any single task yourself than to delegate it. When, on the other hand, your focus is on getting others to follow your lead, getting the right people on board and keeping them there is of surpassingly obvious significance.

So the first step in successful staffing is taking a deep breath and reminding yourself that finding the right employee for an open position doesn't take you away from your job. Quite the opposite: It's the most important item on your to-do list. You and your team will be working with and depending on the result of this process for quite awhile. You need to do it well.

Next, you must unlearn a bit of currently-fashionable nonsense: The Sack O'Skills theory of employee acquisition. According to this theory, employees are passive collections of the skills required for success, so the first stage in recruiting is to prepare a detailed list of objectively measurable skills each candidate must possess in order for their resume to pass through the HR filter and reach your desk.

If you don't peel the onion very far this sounds like a reasonable thing to do: If, for example, you're looking for someone to administer your Oracle database, only consider people who know how to administer Oracle databases. It's so obvious!

Here's why the Sack O'Skills theory is wrong: You're hiring a person, not a resume. You're hiring an employee who, over the course of his or her career, will be asked to take on a wide variety of roles within the organization.

Put it as a syllogism:

My major premise is that the best employees are motivated employees.

My minor premise is that motivated employees generally have career goals – they won't want to retire in the positions for which you're hiring them.

My conclusion is that the best employees have career goals and won't want to retire in the positions they start in.

Nor, by the way, do you want them to. Your need for any particular skill is transient, because technology routinely makes some skills obsolete while at the same time it creates a need for new ones. Do you really want to continually churn your work force to get the right mix of skills? Doing so is expensive, time-consuming, and wasteful. Every time you churn a position you lose valuable knowledge about how things work, de-motivate the employees who remain, and disrupt team dynamics as everyone learns to operate without the old team members and with the new ones.

Beyond these problems, this practice doesn't pass the "Mom Test": What if everyone did this? Answer: Nobody would ever acquire a new skill, and you wouldn't be able to recruit the talent you need anyway.

Your need for any particular skill is transient. If you believe in the Sack O'Skills theory you'll churn your work force constantly to get the skills you need without paying for training.

It will be a mistake. In the long run, character, intelligence, aptitude and judgment are far more important than possession of any narrowly-defined skill. Why? Not because of any ethical consideration, but because these, far more than any skill, determine whether an employee will succeed or fail at the responsibilities you assign.

The short version: If you want employees who succeed, hire employees who know how to succeed.

The conclusion is inescapable: In corporate America the business function most in need of re-engineering is recruiting. The Sack O'Skills approach has Human Resources screening applicants for specific suitability based on a detailed list of identifiable skills, leaving matters of character to the hiring manager, who of course also has to check for real technical competence since HR can't do much more than look for a list of keywords.

Wouldn't it make more sense for HR to screen only for general knowledge of whatever subject matter the job requires, instead concentrating most of its attention on whether the applicant has a track record of achievement, is in the habit of succeeding, and is the kind of person the company wants as an employee?

If HR took on that task, the hiring manager could focus on what he or she knows best – whether the individual will be able to do the job that needs doing, and will be able to grow into the next job that needs doing as well. And will fit into the team that's already in place to get the work done.

You're hiring a person, not a résumé. If all you need is a sack o'skills, hire a contractor or consultant. That's what they're for.

So. You've gone through the effort, carefully screened résumés, interviewed for character, drive and ability, and made a great hire. Great! You're done.

You knew it wasn't that simple, didn't you? You're no more done with staffing when you've hired a new employee than you are done with marketing when a new customer first decides to buy from you. With customers, the key to success is repeat business, as persuading a non-customer to buy from you for the first time costs, on the average, around five times what it costs to persuade a recent customer to buy from you again. That's the central premise of customer relationship management (CRM).

With employees, it can cost as much as a full year's salary to replace a good employee who leaves for another opportunity, once you factor in the cost of recruiting, orientation and training, acculturation, and all the other factors that add up to a lot of lost productivity.

It's worth noting that when you hire a new employee, you're selling the applicant on the desirability of working for you just as much as the applicant is selling you on his or her ability to do the job.

Employees are, or at least should be selling you every day on their ability to do the job they want – that's how they get promoted. And you should be selling them, too – every day – on the desirability of continuing to work for you instead of seeking their fortunes elsewhere. This isn't, by the way, typical 21st century capitalism. Business leaders long-ago jettisoned loyalty as a virtue. But that's just a fashion trend, which means you should no more automatically follow it than you should automatically buy a loud and ugly tie because this year "everyone" is wearing loud and ugly ties.

Industry as a whole long-ago decided to treat employees as fungible commodities – interchangeable sacks o'skills – and employees eventually figured out the logical implications of that change in attitude. That doesn't mean you can't gain the loyalty of your employees, but you have to earn it. The way to do so is to recognize that each employee's first loyalty is to him or herself. Your job is to create a situation where it's in each employee's self-interest ... each good employee's self-interest, that is ... to stay with you.

That's a lot harder than hiring great employees, because it isn't an event.

It's a way of life.

LIKE HIRES LIKE

Every employment coach knows that hiring managers tend to hire those who resemble themselves.

They usually justify the decision with the phrase, "I trusted my gut." Which they did. Usually they would have been better off trusting their gut less and their brains more, since their guts focus more on trivialities like quality of haircut, handshake, and manner of dress than on the ability to get the job done.

When you're looking for a job, remember that people tend to hire themselves. When you're hiring, make sure you don't – instead, look for people whose strengths complement your own.

It doesn't, by the way, begin with compensation. Yes, you have to compensate people fairly (although defining "fairly" is an interesting task) but loyalty isn't something you can buy[7]. (Chapter Five, *Motivation*, covers this subject in more depth.)

It begins by making sure it is in each employee's self-interest to stay, and that each employee understands it that way. You've hired ambitious people with career aspirations. Give each one opportunities to grow, to gain new experiences, skills, and successes. Pay bonuses when they do something extraordinary that delivers tangible value for your organization – not because you want them to feel grateful but because you feel grateful – it's an appropriate response to the circumstance.

Above all, treat them with respect, listen to their ideas rather than simply giving them airtime, and continually persuade them that your organization is where they should want to work.

If experience with customers provides any guidance, it should take only one fifth the effort to retain a great employee than it takes to recruit one. And since failing to retain a great employee means you're going to have to go out and recruit a replacement, isn't this a good investment of your time?

SUMMARY

▶ If leadership is getting others to follow, and to lead on your behalf, then the importance of choosing the best people to do so is clear. Finding the right person to fill an open position isn't a distraction from your job. As a leader, it is your job.

▶ Avoid the Sack O'Skills theory of hiring: Employees aren't just collections of skills and abilities. Employees bring to

---

[7] The reverse doesn't hold: Paying people unfairly will earn their disloyalty for reasons way too obvious to elaborate on.

their work motivation, loyalty, knowledge of the company, and most important of all the ability to drive success.

▸ Hire people who will be able to take on a variety of roles over the course of a career.

▸ To hire effectively, reverse the standard roles of human resources and the hiring manager: Have human resources screen for general domain knowledge and a habit of succeeding at assignments. The hiring managers should screen for specific technical knowledge and the ability to fit in with the other employees already on the team.

▸ Recruit the employees you have even more than the employees you want.

▸ If all you want is a collection of skills and abilities, hire a contractor or consultant – that's what they're for.

CHAPTER FIVE

Motivation

The line that separates motivating employees from manipulating them is thin, and is determined entirely by your intentions.

I once read that it's impossible to motivate employees. The gist of the essay was that all motivation comes from within.

Well, maybe, but then how do you explain the simple observable fact that the employees in some companies are more motivated than in others?

Maybe it's a matter of staffing practices. Or maybe not, because without much effort you can find employees who exhibited strong motivation in one environment, only to become apathetic do-the-minimum drones in another, and vice versa.

It very well may be true that you can't motivate employees. However, even if you can't motivate them you can do something that's nearly indistinguishable from it, which is to discover and nurture the motivation they have inside themselves.

Even more important, it is definitely true that you can (and poor leaders often do) de-motivate employees.

So if you don't want to split hairs, as a leader you're responsible for the level of motivation experienced by your employees. More simply, you gotta get them motivated. The question isn't whether, it's how.

There's no single answer that works for everyone. And thank heavens for that. People are different from each other, so what motivates one will have no effect on another. To effectively motivate people you first have to understand them as individuals. Sure, some charismatic leaders can give an inspiring speech and "motivate" a few thousand or a few million total strangers, but that's a temporary effect.

The motivation that counts has to operate every day, with enough impact to carry employees though the grinding detail that's the difference between grand vision and an accomplished strategy. Which means motivation is a leadership responsibility that must be delegated. Each front-line leader must be responsible for motivation. Higher-level leaders are as well, but more importantly are responsible for delegating the task properly, which includes providing the right tools for getting the job done.

Think of it as the difference between advertising and selling: You can do the former from a distance; the latter is up-close and personal. Both matter, if for no other reason than that good advertising makes the sales representative's job easier.

It's exactly the same when it comes to motivating employees: Good leadership in the executive ranks makes it much easier for front-line supervisors to motivate the employees who report to them.

Before worrying about how to motivate employees, though, it's worth your time to understand what de-motivates them. That's easily done: Just consider what de-motivates you. It's a short, easy list of things to avoid. If you want to de-motivate someone, here are the best ways to do it:

> ▶ *Arrogance:* Make it clear you think you're better or more important than they are.
> ▶ *Disrespect:* The flip side of arrogance – demonstrate

how unimportant you think your employees are to
your company's success, or how incompetent you
think they are.

▶ *Unfairness:* Using compensation as a motivator is
unlikely to succeed, as is explained later on. But it
can be an exceptionally effective de-motivator. Just
compensate unfairly. Especially, ignore performance
and instead reward a good haircut and strong
handshake. (Remember like hiring like in Chapter
Four? It doesn't stop with the hiring process.)

Want a perfect score? Make it clear you consider all
success to be yours and all failure to be your employees' fault,
which is why, during these hard times, you're laying off some
staff, cutting the salaries and eliminating raises for those who
remain, and giving yourself and other executives a bonus for
making the hard decisions. You win the Trifecta: Simultaneous
arrogance, disrespect and unfairness.

Remarkably, this happens all the time. If you read *The Wall
Street Journal*, keep your eyes open. You won't have long to
wait before the next installment.

De-motivating employees is easy. Motivating them is
harder. The good news is, you have several tools at your
disposal – five, to be exact – each suited for different
employees and situations. They're the same five motivators
used by canny marketers and sales professionals to drive
prospects to buy products and services. They can work just as
well for you when the time comes to motivate your
employees.

What are these magical motivators? The need for approval
comes first, followed by exclusivity, fear, greed, and guilt.
Each has its place in your repertoire. They aren't
interchangeable, though: Each is suited to different situations
as well as different employees. Also, each one, used wrong,

can backfire.

Here's how they work.

NEED FOR APPROVAL

Out of all of the motivational tools available to you, this is your workhorse. It isn't too far from the truth to say that you lead those who look to you for approval and you're led by those to whom you look for approval. It's a powerful tool. And like any power tool, it can saw off one of your limbs if you aren't careful .

Not really. When giving people pats on the back there are only a few places you can go wrong. We'll get them out of the way. Everything else is doing it right.

Insincerity: You have to mean it, of course, or else be one hell of an actor. If people think you're insincere, you've simultaneously devalued the approval and their perception of your integrity. If you don't mean it, don't say it.

Low standards: People respond to approval. When they do, you might be tempted to give them more of it. Don't.

B. F. Skinner, the father of behavioral psychology (an occasionally useful discipline although far, far less useful than Skinner thought it was) described a phenomenon in rats called "periodic variable reinforcement." It works like this. If you put a rat in a cage, and reward it with a pellet of food every time it presses a bar, it quickly loses interest. Give the same rat a pellet of food every 10th time it presses the bar, or even better after a random number of presses, and the rat will press the bar just short of forever.

The same phenomenon does work in humans. As evidence I offer slot machines and golf.

So if you compliment people every time they sneeze ("Nice sneeze, Wilbur!") your approval will quickly lose its impact. Compliment them more rarely, and only when they've accomplished something worthy of praise, and they'll work hard to get the next compliment, and glow when it arrives.

THE PARABLE OF AMADEUS

How can you spot the real leader of an organization? It's easy: See who looks to whom for approval.

When you're in a leadership role, one of the most difficult accomplishments is psychological: schooling yourself to not need the approval of others. The extent to which you desire praise is the extent to which you can be led (or manipulated) by anyone willing to give you a compliment.

Which brings up the subject of ego-driven executives. Their need for ego-feeding allows others to influence their decisions through the trick of flattery instead of the use of facts and logic. They're led rather than leading.

In the play Amadeus, the character Salieri wanted to be the most famous composer of his time, while Mozart wanted to be the greatest. Salieri's tragedy was that both got their wishes.

There are many ways people look for approval. While some executives are susceptible to brown-nosing, others, like Salieri, need something else – accolades, whether it's a mention in the business press or an invitation to the White House.

It's pretty simple: An executive who needs such things ... who needs the approval of others ... is, like Salieri, less likely to build something that endures than a leader driven to build a great organization and giving it direction.

Compliment them too rarely and they'll stop trying.

Brown-nosing: The technique of giving approval isn't limited to those who report to you, any more than any other dimension of leadership is limited to that group of people. Providing approval to peers and your own leaders can be an excellent way to establish yourself as first among equals.

Or to establish you as a spineless suck-up.

It's really a matter of attitude as much as anything else. Don't do it too often, do it sincerely, and most important of all, do it as one peer would naturally compliment another. If you aren't certain, compare the situation to a round of golf. "Nice shot, Jim," is perfectly natural when said to a peer, so long as Jim actually hit a nice shot.

Or, think of it this way: Someone who's brown-nosing gives a compliment so as to be noticed and appreciated – in other words, to get approval. Your goal is the opposite: For someone to appreciate the approval you give.

EXCLUSIVITY

Whether you're a bleacher bum in Wrigley Field, on your church's board of directors, a Shriner, or one of the few, the proud, The Marines, chances are one of your reasons for doing so is to feel like you're part of an elite group – to have something that distinguishes you from the Great Unwashed.

The need is unsurprising. On this earth, as of this writing, more than six billion souls compete for air, food and shelter. Many strive for uniqueness as well – it's easy to feel unimportant and redundant when 5,999,999,999 other people will be there to pick up the slack if you were to vanish without a trace.

Perhaps it's because each of us represents a mere 1/6,000,000,000 of humanity (if you're a U.S. citizen, you represent about 1/280,000,000 of the population – feel better?)

that so many people feel the need to be part of some
exclusive group or other.

You can use this desire as a powerful way to motivate
people. How?

Treat each person you lead as a unique individual, that's
how. They'll appreciate it, treasure it, and go the extra mile
for you because of it.

Remember each individual's name and use it. "George, can
I talk to you for a moment?" works much better than "Hey,
you with the face, come over here!"

Remember something about each person. "Hello, Rachel.
Is your daughter over that ear infection you mentioned last
time we spoke?" If Rachel reports to you ... especially if
Rachel reports to someone who reports to you ... your
remembering this tidbit will be significant.

If you aren't convinced, try this: Next time you go out to
eat, pay attention to the server. Remember the server's name,
find out something about him or her. Treat your server as an
individual, not a nameless waitron. Nine times out of ten or
better you'll get service superior to anyone else in the
restaurant.

That's one way to use the need for exclusivity as a
motivator. It's harmless and effective, and creates a bond of
loyalty, so long as you practice it consistently. There's nobody
more irritating and obvious than a guy who's your best friend
whenever he wants something but who doesn't even
acknowledge your existence otherwise. Exclusivity is a
relationship-builder, not a transactional technique.

There's another use for exclusivity that's more dangerous –
a technique that's useful when motivating the team of people
who report to you, or to become first among equals when
interacting with peers, if that's one of your goals. How?
Simple: Portray your team as the elite, better in some way

than the other teams, or at least in competition with the others trying to prove they're better.

It's a cheap, easy trick for creating a sense of cohesion and a desire to excel.

Beware of things that are cheap and easy.

This should be obvious: Every time you tell a team it's the elite, you're telling every other team you think they aren't as good. It's a dangerous message to deliver, for several reasons beyond the obvious one that you've just become a rude boor.

First of all, unless you're planning to end your career in your current position, some of those teams you're disparaging might end up reporting to you. The damage control you'll have to do then is significant – it will be a long time before any of the people whose abilities you downplayed will trust you.

Beyond that, when you promote your team as better than any other team in the company you limit the perception of your scope to your team. In other words, you've made yourself appear small, rather than as someone ready for promotion to broader responsibilities.

Bad career move.

Still, sometimes you're presiding over a death march and the need for esprit de corps outweighs all other considerations. If so, leverage the desire for exclusivity. If works.

Better yet: Cast the elite descriptor over the whole company, focusing your staff's us-vs-them attitude on your company's competitors instead of the department down the hall.

That gives you the best of both words – it motivates your team while painting you as an executive, ready for greater roles in the company.

FEAR

Yoda told young Aniken Skywalker, "Fear leads to anger,

anger leads to hatred, and hatred leads to suffering." Maybe so, but he left out a few steps.

Fear is the most powerful motivator known to man[8]. Fear makes people faster and stronger, gives them more endurance, alerts them to the need to avert imminent and damaging consequences ... and can make them incredibly stupid, too[9].

Under what circumstances should you use fear to motivate an employee? When you need strength and endurance, and most significantly when you need the employee to change in some important and difficult way.

Fear is a perfectly valid motivator when the circumstances are dire. "If we can't get this job done, our chance of surviving as an independent company are pretty low," is a powerful incentive for employees to work harder and for longer hours than they otherwise would, so long as the statement is both true and persuasive.

"If you don't buckle down and start producing, we're going to have to replace you with somebody who will," is an equally valid motivator. There's an old and very true saying that people don't change until they face a life-threatening experience. If you need an employee to make a fundamental change, fear is the exact right tool for the job.

Make sure, though, that employees fear the situation and not you personally. If they fear the situation they'll work hard to avert it. If they fear you they'll work hard to avoid you, and

[8] I'm pretty sure it's the most powerful motivator known to woman as well, but my knowledge of that subject is second-hand at best.

[9] True story: Once, when I was SCUBA diving, the dive master led us to a moray eel's hidey hole without telling us. He thought he was being funny. When the eel shot out of the hole swimming straight at us, my back was turned. This was a very big moray. My dive buddy helpfully yelled, "Behind you! Behind you!" into her regulator but of course it came out sounding more like, "Burble burble burble," before, with incredible speed and power, she swam in the opposite direction. Which shows that fear makes you almost as stupid as testosterone.

communication will be at an end. You can't lead people who don't listen to you and, more importantly, won't give you honest and accurate information. Even worse, they'll never exhibit the most prized trait of all among those whom you lead – followership. They can't – they'll never make decisions based on their own judgment and initiative if they're constantly looking over their shoulders at how you're going to second-guess them.

[Note to Machiavellians – yes, Machiavelli did say that if you have to choose, you're better off being feared than loved. There is, however, a big difference between "better" and "good." When people report to you it's wise to make sure they know you can make hard decisions. It's wise to make sure they know you aren't afraid to use your authority. Maintaining the difference between being friendly and being their friend – as in peer – is important to defining your relationship with those who report to you. It's one thing to make sure they know you're capable of decisions they'd rather not experience, quite another to regularly use fear as a motivator.]

Just remember – fear gives people strength and stamina. It also makes them hasty, intemperate, irritable, irascible, impatient ... yes, and it impairs their judgment as well. Only use fear as a motivator if you're willing to live with the tradeoff.

GREED

Connect the dots: Love of money is the root of all evil. Our entire economy is built on the desire for wealth. We call economies predicated on the assumption of personal altruism "communism" and describe them as godless and evil.

Huh?

Whether or not the desire to accumulate wealth (or to live the lifestyle wealth provides) is evil, our economy is built on the assumption that this is a primary motivator for most citizens. Therefore, we should be able to motivate employees by promising to satisfy that desire, shouldn't we?

Not so fast. The situation is far, far more complicated than that. Most Americans would enjoy being wealthy. That's why so many buy lottery tickets despite the odds. For most, though, the desire for wealth reaches a point of diminishing returns once the cost of acquiring that wealth becomes apparent.

Most, in other words, want a life, too, so once their income provides the standard of living they aspire to, greed ceases to be enough of a motivator to do an effective job.

There's another limitation to using greed as a motivator: Every time you satisfy it, that level of satisfaction immediately becomes an entitlement. People don't like to feel a sense of obligation, so once the initial rush of gratitude has passed, most decide that whatever you gave them is something they deserved.

Probably, you explained it that way, too.

Which means the next time they do whatever it was you rewarded them for, they'll expect the same level of reward again. Want them to exceed their past performance? Fine, but then they'll expect a greater reward next time.

That's just one of the problems with greed as a motivator. Here's another, specific to using salary increases as a way to motivate higher performance: Raises are annuities. If I perform well for a year and you increase my salary as a form of reward, I continue to receive the increase even if my performance plummets to previously unimaginable lows. If you don't believe me, look at how many professional sports figures were superstars before negotiating an eight-figure salary but bums afterward.

The mechanics of compensation systems are important,

but they aren't leadership issues, which puts them outside of this book's scope. Here, it's enough to say that in the long run it's unlikely your compensation system will prove satisfactory as a motivational tool, but it's very easy to turn it into a de-motivating system.

All you gotta do is pay people for one thing while telling them you want something different. That makes you a hypocrite, and there isn't much that's more de-motivating than that.

GUILT

What are you, their mother? Guilt is the motivator used by passive-aggressive personalities. There might be a place for it in a business setting.

There might, but I doubt it.

ISN'T ACHIEVEMENT A PRIMARY MOTIVATIONAL TOOL?

So far, this chapter has focused on techniques you can use to motivate employees. The best employees, though, are driven by the desire to achieve something important. Shouldn't that be the first and most important motivator?

In a word, no.

Beyond any shadow of a doubt, your best employees are wired this way. All you need to do for them is to give them opportunities to achieve something important. After that, your job will be keeping up with them.

It's also true that the desire to achieve important results is built into most employees. As you help each employee develop, one of your most important goals should be to help each one recognize this inner drive and nurture it.

To accomplish this, though, you need to use the primary motivators, and in particular the needs for approval and exclusivity.

For most employees, the desire to achieve must be developed – it's an end, not a starting point.

It is, however, a very desirable end. When you hire employees, look for the desire to achieve. When you promote employees, promote those who demonstrate a desire and ability to achieve. When you talk about the traits you value, place this one first.

Of course.

SUMMARY

▶ Leaders can motivate employees. They also can de-motivate them. Given the immense value of the former, the prevalence of the latter is mystifying.

▶ The primary de-motivators are arrogance, disrespect, and unfairness. Avoid them.

▶ The primary motivators are the *need for approval, exclusivity, fear, greed, and guilt*. Each has its own dynamics – its advantages and pitfalls:

▷ The *need for approval* is the most useful motivational tool at a leader's disposal. Most employees cherish the sincere approval of a leader and will work hard and smart to get it. Strike the right balance – be neither so demanding that your approval is impossible to obtain, nor so easily pleased that it's meaningless. Also, be aware of your own need for approval: Those you need it from end up leading you, even if they report to you.

▷ *Exclusivity* is powerful but dangerous. Most people want to be part of a small, elite group. That's the good news. The bad news: The easiest way to satisfy this desire is to foster a sense of competition between your team and other teams inside the company. Don't do this – as a leader, you're responsible for the whole company, not just your part of the organizational chart.

▷ *Fear* creates energy and stamina, but makes employees stupid. Fear should, for the most part, be about the situation, not about the leader, because fear of the leader kills followership.

▷ *Greed* is limited in its usefulness for most employees. It becomes an entitlement too quickly; also, it creates the uneasy sense that you're trying to bribe them to perform. Financial rewards are better viewed as the loudest and most sincere message a company can send than as a motivator of performance.

▷ *Guilt* has no place in a professional setting.

▷ The *desire to achieve* is, for those employees who have it, the most powerful motivator of all. It is, however, not directly accessible. As a leader you have to cultivate and nurture it. If you can do so successfully, it makes everything else much easier.

CHAPTER SIX

Building and maintaining teams

Groups can't become teams
unless their members are interdependent.

In a team, we're all smarter than any of us are, or so the saying goes. It's true, within limits, so long as you remember that in a group, we're all stupider.

The world of business has no shortage of junk theory. There are days, in fact, when the world of commerce looks like a gigantic junk-theory repository. Sorting and ranking it all to identify the single worst junk theory is an overwhelming task.

So I won't tell you that when the sales force assembles for a pep rally and the director of sales refers to the assembled multitude as the "sales team", it's the worst junk theory of them all.

Or maybe I will. It's barely possible there's a worse junk theory lurking somewhere in the junk-theory warehouse, waiting for some junk-theory mining tool to discover it. But I doubt it.

My dictionary defines "team" thusly: "A number of persons associated in some joint action, esp. one of the sides in a match: *a team of football players.*"

It isn't a team, in other words, unless the individuals involved are interdependent. If any one team member can accomplish the team's goals without the help of any other team member – if, that is, teamwork isn't required for success – you don't have a team.

It's easy to misunderstand this point, and lots of managers do. They try to make teamwork mandatory instead of unavoidable. They mark down excellent employees on performance reviews for "not being a team player" even though the employee gets the job done perfectly. If an employee can get the job done without asking anyone else for help, they've saved you money! Why on earth should this be a negative?

A football team is a team because there's no way one player can score, or prevent the other team from scoring, by himself. The same thing is true in a software development team.

It isn't, however, true of most call centers. So if you want your staff to function as a team, organize the work so that teamwork is unavoidable. Otherwise, recognize that you don't and won't have a team.

Getting back to junk theories, I suppose a few companies may have organized their sales professionals in a way that encourages joint action. Maybe. But think about the dynamics of most sales organizations: Sales representatives have defined territories to prevent their coming into professional contact with each other; they operate independently, and they compete with each other for prizes.

Not the stuff of teamwork.

The word "team" has been mightily abused in the halls of business. Any time a bunch of people are in a room together, they're a "team", except that they rarely are anything of the kind.

The dynamics of groups and the dynamics of teams have nothing to do with each other except that they're opposites:

Teams have that overused term "synergy[10]"; groups have whatever the opposite of synergy is. Dysergy? Antergy? Dysentery?

Groups, in other words, are the same as teams in the sense that black is the same as white only darker. Or as K said to J in *Men in Black*, "A person is smart. People are dumb, panicky, dangerous animals." Groups are dangerous, placid and hard to move at best, easily transformed into mobs at worst.

Why is that?

It's because teamwork is an unnatural act, which only arises under very special circumstances. It's wonderful when it happens, and what's even more wonderful is that true leaders are able to evoke it in the people they lead. It is, however, an unnatural act. To understand why this is true, we'll start with a situation explored by the mathematician Jon Von Neumann called "The Prisoner's Dilemma."

Von Neumann invented the field of mathematics called Game Theory. He imagined two prisoners being interrogated separately for a crime. Each is told that if he cooperates, he'll get off with a light penalty, maybe a year in a minimum security facility, while the other prisoner gets a stiff sentence – maybe five years in the slammer. The reverse is also true. The prisoners both know that if neither informs on the other, they'll both go free. If they both rat? They both get the minimum security sentence[11].

Hence the dilemma. You can almost hear a prisoner's thoughts: *"If I talk, I get a slap on the wrist. If I keep my mouth shut, I either go free or do hard time. And my partner*

---

[10] Arthur Koestler, who popularized the term in his book, *Beyond Reductionism*, wanted it to describe circumstances under which one and one add up to something more than two. The dictionary definition merely requires cooperation. On those rare occasions when you see the term in this book, it's in the Koestlerian sense.

[11] Game theorists have explored a wide variety of payoffs; this is just one possibility.

*is in the same boat – what's he going to do? I bet he's going to
rat on me – he doesn't have what it takes to gut it out. I have
no choice – if I rat I get off easy but if I keep my trap shut I'm
almost sure to be thrown in the slammer! I'd better talk."*

In the Prisoner's Dilemma, cooperation is better for both
prisoners, but the chances of it happening are tiny. And that's
a two person game. Now think of the sales force. What are
they thinking about?

*"If I'm a team player and anyone else in the room works
solo, that's the SOB who will win the trip to Hawaii. To heck
with that!"*

When we're in a team we're all smarter than any of us are.
When we're in a group, we're all stupider. What makes a team
smart?

Let's start with a question that's measurably simpler ... a
question that's 20% shorter: "What makes a team?" This is a
good thing to know, because if you know what makes a team
you have at least some chance of turning the rag-tag band of
rugged individuals who report to you into one.

If you've never watched *The Dirty Dozen*, rent the DVD.
It's the story of a bunch of hardened military criminals, turned
into a crack squad of commandos by ultimate tough guy Lee
Marvin, who as Major John Reisman understood the nature of
teams better than any management consultant.

So instead of a bunch of theory, we're going to learn from
the master in the real-world environment of *The Dirty Dozen*[12].

Okay, you're Major John Reisman and you have to turn
these psychopaths into a team. What's the first thing you do?

The first thing Reisman did was to define a common, clear,
tangible goal ... in this case, to kill a castlefull of Nazi high
brass. Teams need shared goals, or if you need to charge for

---

[12] Hey, I thought it was very realistic!

this wisdom, "common objectives"[13]. That's why the dreaded Mission Statement is integral to team formation. (Please note that Reisman didn't involve his team in defining the mission, nor did anyone worry very much about the details of its phrasing.)

For a team to form, its members must find the goal important. Ideally, the importance will be intrinsic – everyone will want it to happen because it will be a *good thing*. Sometimes, the goal lacks intrinsic value to the team, as was the case in the movie. That's okay – while adoption of the goal will be slower, you can use a team's natural competitiveness, or the quality of the challenge itself, to elevate the goal to importance over time.

A tangible, valuable reward came next: Reisman offered amnesty for every team member on completion of the mission. Since the alternative was staying in the stockade until execution, this reward was pretty significant.

The subject of rewards is complex. If all you do is to say, "Get the job done and there's a bonus in it for you," in effect you're trying to bribe employees to work hard[14]. There's nothing particularly immoral about this, but you risk turning an incentive into an entitlement. Once bonuses have become entitlements, you're lost. Your employees will become resentful and demoralized if they don't get their bonus, even if they've done nothing to deserve them.

It's easiest when you're leading a project. If the team completes the project on time, on budget, and delivering a complete set of high-quality deliverables, it gets an immediate, significant pile of cash. It's easiest because the reward is

---

[13] A synonymous phrase containing 250% more syllables.

[14] Credit where it's due: Alfie Kohn is the originator of this line of thought. Read *Punished by Rewards: The Trouble with Gold Stars, Incentive Plans, A's, Praise, and Other Bribes* (Houghton Mifflin, 1993).

closely and clearly tied to the achievement. Psychologically, a reward tied to an accomplishment is unlikely to turn into an entitlement. Yes, employees will expect another bonus the next time they achieve an important result, as they should. That's different: It's an "entitlement" when you feel you deserve whatever it is because you consume oxygen and display a pulse.

Not all teams are project-based, though. The ones that aren't end up with annual goals and annual bonuses. It's hard to keep an annual bonus from becoming an entitlement for the simple reason that it's on a schedule. The solution?

It isn't easy, and there's no magic formula. The key is tying bonuses to both achievement of the goal and individual contribution to achievement of the goal. If you give someone a bonus because he or she performed well even though the team failed to achieve its goals, you encourage team members to put their individual goals above the team's goals, providing a disincentive for teamwork. If you give every team member the same bonus, you provide a disincentive for individual hard work.

Done right, annual bonuses will vary from year to year, from employee to employee, and from team to team. They will be big enough to be important to the people who receive them. They'll have a clear linkage to individual and team performance. And they'll have one more characteristic: Clear linkage to the value the team has created. This is what keeps a bonus from becoming a bribe. Psychologically, there's a big difference between telling an employee, "Your work resulted in a lot of new revenue for the company, and you deserve to share in those results," and "We want you to work hard so we'll pay you extra if you do."

There's one more point worth making on this subject before getting back to Major John Reisman: Don't even try to use salary increases as performance incentives. You'll never succeed, and you'll breed cynicism in the attempt. Why? Because incentives must be big enough to matter to their recipients, that's why, and salary increases never are.

Do the math. Imagine the median pay for a particular job function is $50K per year. Also imagine you give poor performers no raise at all, average performers 4%, and top performers 8%. You might think the differences are enough to provide an incentive – after all, $4,000 is a significant piece of change for someone who's earning $50K.

But they aren't. Assuming employees receive paychecks twice a month, after all deductions have been removed top performers will take home about fifty bucks per paycheck more than average ones. Ask yourself if that's enough to justify busting your hump.

There's another factor that makes using raises as incentives even worse: A raise is an annuity – perform well this year and you're rewarded for it forever. What kind of sense does that make?

Here's the good news: Because bonuses aren't annuities, if you shift performance rewards from salary increases to bonuses the amount involved can be about three times bigger – a $4,000 raise corresponds to a $12,000 bonus. That's an amount employees will find interesting.

So instead of using salaries as incentives, just index them to inflation. Use the consumer price index and compensation surveys as reference points, and adjust salary to whichever is bigger. (If CPI is bigger and you don't at least match it, you'll pay employees less this year than last – a huge demoralizer. If compensation surveys lead to the bigger number and you don't match the marketplace, good employees will have an incentive to leave.)

The other time you change an employee's salary, of course,

is when the employee receives a promotion, either to a new job, or a new level of competence within a job function. That, of course, is just another version of keeping compensation in line with market rates.

Major John Reisman didn't have to worry about these complexities, of course. He was leading a project team, offering them a clear, tangible, reward for achieving the project's goals. That's all he needed to do on the subject of rewards.

It wasn't all he had to do to make the dirty dozen an effective team, though. The next step in making this happen was to put them in situations where they had to cooperate to achieve difficult objectives. A lot of companies like to do this by putting people in the wilderness where they have to climb cliffs and catch trout together with a bent paper clip. Personally, I don't think much of this approach, because it has *nothing at all to do with cooperation in the workplace.*

Context is everything, and the dirty dozen had to cooperate in training exercises relevant to the work they were going to have to do. If you have a group you're trying to turn into a team, consider scenario-based team training, where the team has to work together in a simulated, facilitated facsimile of the real-world tasks they'll be undertaking together.

For example, I once launched a process redesign team by putting it through methodology training together. The methodology training process had us redesign the process of making burgers in a fast food joint as a team. In the process we got a sense of how each other thought, worked, and interacted.

And yes, it worked quite well.

So if you're leading network support (for example) and you want the group to function as a team, put the team through troubleshooting exercises. Create a problem in your test LAN, perhaps, and let the team fix it. Watch as they do so, and debrief at the end to let the team figure out how it could do things better next time.

The teamwork you've helped create will be far more enduring than group trout-catching.

Reisman used one other, very important technique in turning the dirty dozen into a team: Creating a sense of team identity. He did so by letting the team choose its own leader – John Cassavetes, in the role of Victor Franko, who assumed the mantle of team leadership by fomenting a minor rebellion. Franko got the team to refuse to bathe or shave.

Reisman, rather than enforcing his own rules regarding personal hygiene, let the team make this choice, turning it into the "dirty dozen" by doing so.

Now pay attention: Reisman didn't create the team's sense of identity, nor did he try to be part of the team. Teams must find their own sense of identity and their own internal leadership. The appointed leader must maintain some distance, because that's part of what's needed to maintain authority. Even among the most employee-empowered workplace, appointed leaders must maintain their authority or they become completely ineffective.

This is, by the way, one reason it's hard for "doers" to become leaders – their instinct is to take on some of the work themselves, but in doing so they become part of the team as opposed to its external leader. It's possible to do both, but it's tricky. If you're in a leadership role and have to make a choice, err on the side of distance and delegate the task. Pitch in when the situation requires it, but make that an exception you reserve for emergencies.

There's another factor in team dynamics every leader has to recognize: Too much focus on the mission is self-defeating. Teams have to maintain themselves, and the way they do so is through banter, bull sessions, joke-telling, and lots of other apparently unproductive activity. The dirty dozen interacted with each other socially, and it did so *on company time!* Let this happen. It will anyway, and if you try to stop it you'll just get frustrated.

WHAT MAKES A TEAM?

When you first assemble a group it lacks the two defining characteristics of a team: Alignment, and trust. Even if everyone is committed to the team's goal, it isn't really aligned because different team members will think about the goal differently. When a team first forms, its members' understanding of the goal is one-dimensional, their trust of each other is superficial, and their communication is hampered by a common vocabulary that lacks common semantics.

To put it another way: Everyone thinks they have the same goal, but they don't, and everyone thinks they understand each other, but they don't.

There are well-understood stages of team formation. Generally, they're given the sadly hokey names of "forming, storming, norming, and performing.[15]" It's a simple sequence.

The team starts out with uninformed enthusiasm, bred of ignorance of each other and the goal. As it starts its work, its members discover they aren't working to a common objective after all, and mutual trust plummets. The lack of trust and realization that there's no common goal creates conflict.

This stage is natural and unavoidable. The best you can do is to prepare everyone for it when the team first forms, so they recognize and welcome it. As a team member once asked me, "Did we just reach the storming phase?" When I answered

[15] Don't blame me. Blame Tuckman, B. S., 1965. Developmental Sequences in Small Groups. Psychological Bulletin, vol. 63: pp. 384-399

in the affirmative he seemed relieved – he understood this meant we were making progress.

Usually, a team will work through these issues, achieving common semantics and alignment. In doing so it rebuilds trust levels, this time on the more solid basis of having experienced each other under stress.

What makes a team? High levels of goal alignment and high levels of trust.

Now … back to the earlier question. What makes a team smart?

It's nearly a mathematical necessity that if you pool all of the knowledge, experience, judgment, creativity, and ideas available from every member of a group, you'll end up with more of them all than you'd get from any individual member. Each team member knows something or will think of something nobody else would have come up with.

In a group, there's little alignment and less trust. Each individual wants to get his or her own way on things. The lack of alignment means when I get my way, the group accomplishes my goals instead of everyone else's goals, and since different members have different goals, your ideas don't mean very much to me.

With shared goals, I get value when you have a good idea. It's the receptivity of every team member to the potential contributions of all the others that makes a team smart. It provides an avenue for pooling the abilities of all of the team's members.

Which is exactly why a group is stupider than any of its members, each of whom ends up blocking each other's knowledge and ideas.

Turning a collection of individuals into a team is hard work. It requires patience, expertise, judgment, and will. Since it combines goal-creation and alignment with effective delivery, it is probably the most important function of leadership.

So go out there and win one for the Gipper.

SUMMARY

▶ A collection of individuals isn't a team unless its members must cooperate for each one to achieve success. This rarely happens by accident.

▶ A team must have a common goal. It isn't enough for a leader to state the goal, either: Team members must internalize it and make it their own. In other words, they must be aligned.

▶ Rewards are a risky way to align team members to a common goal. They'll be perceived as bribes, and quickly turn into entitlements. Proper use of compensation and rewards is a complex and difficult exercise.

▶ To form, team members must get in the habit of cooperating, which is best accomplished through contextually relevant exercises held in a controlled environment.

▶ Teams must form their own sense of identity and establish their own internal leadership. Managers have a limited role to play in this process – they should create an atmosphere in which it can happen, but they can't cause it to happen.

▶ Teams require "maintenance" – informal activity and conversation that allows team members to understand each other and build trust.

▶ Appointed leaders shouldn't try to be part of the team. They need some distance to maintain authority.

▶ Teams progress through four stages, defined by the level of trust and alignment among their members. The common names for these stages are "forming, storming, norming, and performing."

▶ Teams are smarter than the individuals that compose them because the knowledge and ideas of all members are pooled. Groups are stupider than the individuals that compose them because the individuals compete, interfering with each other's ability to promote the best ideas.

CHAPTER SEVEN

Culture

*The only way to change the business culture
is to change your own behavior.*

"To change the culture," explained a friend and mentor in the business of business change, "you can either change the people or change the people."

It sounded like a wisecrack but it wasn't: You can either change the people, which is to say find ways to encourage the attitudes and behaviors you're looking for, or you can change the people, replacing those displaying attitudes and behaviors with others who dislay those you do want.

Except that it won't help. You can swap out employees all day long, and if the behavior of your organization's leaders doesn't change, your corporate culture won't change.

It can't.

If you want to understand a subject, go to the source, and for the subject of culture, no discipline has explored it more thoroughly than the one known as cultural anthropology. Cultural anthropologists define culture as the behavior people exhibit in response to their environment. It's a good definition for scientific investigation. Behavior is observable, where the other stuff of culture – rules, knowledge, attitudes and such – must be inferred. It's restricted in scope just enough to be useful as well: It deals only with behaviors that are in response to an individual's environment, not all behaviors of any kind.

So by this definition, to change corporate culture you can either change how employees respond to their environment,

THE REST OF THE EMPLOYEE ENVIRONMENT

"But," you might be objecting, "not every aspect of an employee's environment is the behavior of other employees." And you'd be right. You have some tools for culture change at your disposal that don't require you to alter your employees' attitudes and behaviors.

Two recent examples are the personal computer and its follow-up technology, electronic mail. Each helped drive reductions in formality, more open communication, and greater empowerment of line employees in many organizations. To a certain extent they may have contributed to a reduction in gender-based discrimination as well: By drastically reducing the number of secretaries and typists ... traditionally, female-dominated positions ... they likely reduced the expectation that female employees were secretaries and typists, which in proportion increased the expectation that female employees were peers.

These weren't planned culture changes, though – they happened by accident, and subversively as well. It seems quite likely that had corporate executives known that these consequences would occur, they would have rejected the technologies out of hand.

And even if not ... unpredictable change just isn't as useful as changes you can design and make happen.

or you can change the environment they respond to. Most of the environment each employee is responding to is the behavior of every other employee. Which means to change the culture, you have to change the behavior employees exhibit in response to the behavior employees exhibit in response to the behavior employees exhibit in response ...

Get the picture? At first glance, culture change appears to be a case of infinite regression, intractable and unsolvable. But it isn't as hopeless as all that.

It's worse. Far from being a case of infinite regression, the regression involved in culture change is seriously finite.

It starts with you. You ... specifically your behavior and reactions ... are part of the environment everyone around you responds to.

Okay, that did sound like a paragraph from one of those annoying, inspirational books you bought this book instead of. Sorry.

But it is unavoidably true. As a leader, you represent a disproportionate component of the environment of those employees in your organization. Change your behavior and you change a bunch of their environment. Change the behavior of the leaders who report to you and their environment changes dramatically – you will have changed the culture.

It's that easy. And that hard.

Well, not really. You also might want to spend a few minutes thinking through how you want the culture to change. You might even want to engage your leadership team in addressing the question. After all, you'll be asking them to change their behavior. They should have some say in what it's supposed to be in the future.

So ask them. And recognize that if you're intent on seriously changing the culture of your organization, many of them won't make the cut. If they could, they'd be behaving as "leaders of the future" already, because most people are who they are and aren't going to change just because you say they're supposed to.

Unless they aren't leading that way because of your actions and reactions.

Which leads to an important question: Are you sure you want to go through with this? Because it won't be all that easy for you to change your behavior, either.

* * *

Still here? That must mean you do plan to change your behavior. Good for you. What are you planning to change?

Go back: As with any design process, you should be methodical. So pull your leadership team together and go through an orderly thought process:

- ▶ Describe what about the culture you have you want to preserve.
- ▶ Describe what about your culture you want to change, and what you want it to change into.
- ▶ Shorten the second list to something manageable (at most five items to change; three is better).
- ▶ Decide how you and your team will
  - ▷ Behave differently.
  - ▷ Hold yourselves accountable.
  - ▷ Communicate the desired changes to your organization.
  - ▷ Hold employees accountable.

Note that this process doesn't include creating a full description of either your current culture or the future one. You could, I suppose. Certainly, there are ways to characterize a culture, and you might find value in a consulting study that gives you a full description of your current culture.

More likely, though, what you'd get would be a fascinating

exercise in urban anthropology, not a practical course of action.

So instead:

Get your leaders together and spend no more than a half hour listing what you like about the current culture that shouldn't change, and what you dislike about the current culture that has to change.

While you're at it, make sure you understand why it has to

SUBCULTURES

It's easy to get so wrapped up in defining culture that you forget something obvious: A complex society ... and an information technology department is definitely a very complex society ... doesn't consist of a single, homogeneous culture. It's composed of a collection of subcultures. In a healthy society these subcultures share enough elements to provide social cohesion, but have unique characteristics as well. In an unhealthy society the cohesion breaks down and all that matters are the differences.

Think about your IT organization and you'll immediately recognize any number of subcultures: Applications vs operations; Windows vs Unix vs mainframe; object-oriented developers vs COBOL programmers.

As a leader, your role is to focus on the shared elements that provide cohesion. Just don't try to stamp out the subcultures. They're valuable so long as they don't drive fragmentation and internal rivalry, just as it's valuable for you to create a unique IT subculture within the overall company culture.

change. Which is to say, connect your likes and dislikes to business goals and not just your personal preferences. The purpose of a cultural shift isn't to adjust your environment to maximize your personal comfort. It's to create the optimal environment for achieving your purposes.

Once you know what you and your team think is the right answer, fan out through your chain of command to acquire similar lists from every workgroup in your organization[16].

What kinds of traits are you looking for? Here's a list of random examples:

- ▶ In a crisis we all pull together and don't worry about who's supposed to have which roles and responsibilities.
- ▶ Everyone does whatever they feel like without consulting the experts who are responsible for a function.
- ▶ When an end-user complains about us to someone else they know in IT, what they hear back is how inept our group is.
- ▶ When someone in the business raises an issue about IT's performance we do a very good of listening to them, conveying our concern, and avoiding sounding defensive about it.
- ▶ Everyone really cares about the problems we face.
- ▶ I hear a lot of complaining from my co-workers, but not much in the way of solutions.
- ▶ As far as taking care of the basics is concerned, we're very good at doing things by the numbers. We're disciplined about following well-documented procedures.

[16] Or, if you want to make your ulterior-motive-driven author happy, hire an outside consultant to facilitate this exercise. It isn't a bad thought, either. Using an outside consultant to facilitate this kind of discussion without any managers in the room will usually result in greater candor than having your managers lead the exercise.

▶ We're too bureaucratic. Everything we do is by the book, whether or not the book is a good fit for what the situation calls for.

▶ We say we reach a consensus in a meeting, but after the meeting people do whatever they did before if they don't like the decision.

▶ We're very good at involving everyone when making decisions so that everyone has buy-in.

▶ Our employees are very good at covering the bases and documenting their work to make doubly sure everything goes smoothly.

▶ There's far too much CYK[17] around here.

These are just some examples of what you might uncover in determining the current state of the culture.

If you didn't notice, the above list includes only six characteristics, not twelve. The only difference between each pair of statements is whether the recorder happens to like or dislike the behavior in question. As you and the rest of the leadership team review your culture, pay attention to how each individual phrases his or her likes and dislikes – it's illuminating.

With your leadership team, review the list and decide which behaviors are, in your eyes, positive characteristics for the organization you want to establish. Phrase these in the most positive light you can. Take, for example this pair of statements:

▶ As far as taking care of the basics is concerned, we're very good at doing things by the numbers. We're disciplined about following well-documented procedures.

▶ We're too bureaucratic. Everything we do is by the

---

[17] Cover Your Keister.

book, whether or not the book is a good fit for what the situation calls for.

If you decide you like the underlying thought, here's what might go into the Things We Do Well list:

We're disciplined in how we go about our work. We make use of well-documented processes and procedures. We adhere to them instead of reinventing the wheel every time we need something round, and improve them whenever we see the opportunity to do so.

What about the ones you want to change? Take this pair:

▸ We say we reach a consensus in a meeting, but after the meeting people do whatever they did before if they don't like the decision.

▸ We're very good at involving everyone when making decisions so that everyone has buy-in.

The questions are, how do you want to fix it, and how do you avoid the law of unintended consequences? Luckily, having read Chapter Three on decision-making, you know just how to deal with this one:

When making decisions we will be deliberate, yet decisive. We will consult those whose expertise will enhance the quality of our decisions and involve those whose stake in the result is significant. We will trust the competence and intentions of those who make decisions we aren't part of, and only revisit decisions once we've made them if we have new information that could invalidate our earlier analysis.

One thing to notice: These aren't particularly brief. This is just your loyal author's opinion: While mission and vision statements should be brief, simple, and to the point, cultural descriptions should be thoughtful and balanced. Which behaviors are right and which ones are wrong depends on the context. Your aim should be to help employees find the right balance. That takes more than a five word sentence.

Which leaves us with one more topic for this chapter: How do you and your team need to change in order to achieve the desired shift in culture?

Here's my answer: How well do you trust each other?

LEADERSHIP TEAM CULTURE

Count on this: You can't achieve a planned change in culture without a leadership team whose members trust and rely on each other. Among the many reasons, this one stands out: You need to be able to help each other see each other's foibles, idiosyncrasies, and peculiarities, especially when they act as barriers to achieving the desired culture.

Too often, leaders achieve this need for trust among their direct reports by sacrificing excellence. They choose people whose primary talent is getting along. But as Chico Marx used to say, "Atsa no good."

People whose focus is on getting along rarely raise important issues if they think the issue might cause discomfort or offense ... which is the case with every issue of any importance.

Which leads to one cultural trait to encourage in your leadership team:

We will be brutally honest with each other when discussing any issue of importance ... but our focus will always be on the issue, not on each other.

Issues must be raised to be addressed, and it's mighty rare that issues take care of themselves otherwise. Usually, they fester and get worse.

What else is required for members of a leadership team to trust and rely on each other?

Here's one of the most common mistakes leaders make:

They take the organizational chart too seriously. Look at any organizational chart. What you're seeing is an account of what everyone's responsibility isn't. It's a set of boxes within which managers live their professional lives.

Which leads to a huge recurring problem in many leadership teams: The assumption that if I take care of my part of the organization and Sam over there takes care of his, and we both do our jobs well, then the whole organization will do well.

From the perspective of management theory, this is convincing. But management theory generally ignores minor matters like human nature. It's a mechanical approach to thinking about organizational issues. From a leadership perspective, this attitude is a disaster. Why?

Okay, my responsibility is to ensure that my organization succeeds. That puts me in competition with my peers – for resources, for process optimization, and even in terms of the basic measures through which I define success. Think no further than your company's annual budget wars if you don't believe me.

What's the alternative?

Each member of the leadership team is a leader of the whole organization, accountable for the success of the entire organization. The business functions each of us manages are our current area of focus, not the limit of our responsibilities.

Nothing needs to change to accomplish this except attitude. Oh, and maybe an overhaul of how you calculate bonuses.

If the members of your leadership team can't trust and rely on each other, don't begin to try changing the culture of the rest of your organization. After all, if you can't deal with the culture of a six-person team, what makes you think you can deal with the vastly greater scope of your whole IT organization?

If the members of your leadership team do trust and rely on each other, the rest is relatively straightforward: Help each other see when you aren't setting the right example. If Sam has a habit of revisiting decisions that have already been made, take Sam aside and tell him so. If Bertha frequently asks the dreaded "didja"[18] question of subordinates to whom decisions have been delegated, point it out and recommend the better alternative: She should say, "Tell me how you went about making this decision."

One of my favorite bits of poetry is Robert Burns' famous, *"Would that gift the giftie gie us/To see ourselves as others see us."* To change your culture, you all have to be the giftie.

SUMMARY

▶ Business culture is the behavior employees exhibit in response to their environment. Most of their environment is the behavior of other employees. So culture is the behavior employees exhibit in response to the behavior employees exhibit in response to the behavior …

▶ You can't change how employees respond. Most of their environment is how other employees respond. What you can change is your own behavior – the only real lever you have to change culture. The behavior of your direct reports – the leadership team – is also something you can directly influence.

▶ Culture should be intentional – something you design. The basic steps:

  ▷ Describe what about the culture you have you want to preserve.

---

[18] "Didja think of this? Didja think of that? Didja consider this option too?" Didja turns presentations and recommendations into cross examinations.

▷ Describe what about your culture you want to change, and what you want it to change into.
▷ Shorten the second list to something manageable (at most five items to change; three is better).
▷ Decide how you and your team will
> Behave differently.
> Hold yourselves accountable.
> Communicate the desired changes to your organization.
> Hold employees accountable.
▷ Make sure the culture you design advances your business goals, rather than simply creating the environment you would find most comfortable.

▶ The design of the new culture should be a high-involvement, consultative process. Ask everyone what they like and dislike about the current culture, and use that to help you and your leadership team decide what to change.

▶ Culture change requires trust and commitment on the part of the leadership team. It also requires a shared attitude that every member of the leadership team is a leader of the whole organization, not just their part of the organizational chart.

CHAPTER EIGHT

Communication

*The ability to communicate is the glue that holds all
of the other leadership responsibilities together*

According to conventional wisdom, leaders are
communicators. The conventional wisdom is right. The only
problem is that while it's right, the conventional wisdom is
frequently misunderstood. These misunderstandings have left
us with a bunch of management motor-mouths who Just Won't
Shut Up!

Talking certainly is part of communication. It is, however,
only one part of it. Communication consists of three distinct,
yet interconnected skills: Persuasion, information-sharing, and
listening. Effective leaders excel at all three. They have to.

The ability to communicate is the glue that holds all of the
other leadership responsibilities together: Envisioning the
future, delegation, making decisions and all the rest. To lead,
and to persuade others to lead on your behalf, you have to
communicate.

Persuasion is the logical starting point. In order to lead
you have to do more than get other people to follow you. A
loud voice is, after all, sufficient for that. As Chapter Two
pointed out, what you need is followership – for people to
lead on your behalf. Everything stems from that basic fact.
That's why you need to persuade, and not just bark orders:

Nobody will lead on your behalf unless you persuade them that doing so is a good idea. That's what persuasion is: Getting people to do as you want them to do. Persuasion is the essence of leadership.

When they do follow you, where are they supposed to go? If they're supposed to lead on your behalf, how are they supposed to show initiative in ways that advance your program? People need information to do this – clear, unambiguous information that helps them make effective decisions.

Okay, so far so good – it's clear why you need to talk. Talking is good. When a leader talks and his followers listen, his ego soars like a hot air balloon[19]. But what does listening accomplish?

Does this even need to be said? Leaders should listen for the same reason everyone else should listen: to avoid being ignorant.

That's the overview. Let's dive a bit deeper to make it clear how effective communicators stay smart, keep those who follow them smart, and keep everyone moving in the same direction. Let's start with avoiding ignorance.

LISTENING

Is it worth more than a paragraph to explain why listening is an important part of communicating?

Probably not. While it isn't completely true that you learn nothing when you talk (the act of planning how to explain something does increase your depth of understanding), it certainly is true that you're more likely to acquire new information by listening to others than by their listening to you.

---

[19] I'm tempted to crack wise, but really, what would be the point?

There are leaders who think staff-level employees ... the ones who interact with customers and vendors every day, who wrestle with business applications to get them to do what they're supposed to do, who take the swim-lane diagrams beloved of business process redesigners and turn them into actual work, and who otherwise keep the business running while leaders spend their time trying to turn the organization into something different and better ... have no useful information to share. Just in case you're one of them, you're wrong [20].

Chapter Three introduced the five ways leaders make decisions. You'll recall consultative decision-making was the best general-purpose style of the bunch, providing a reasonable tradeoff between speed, effort and quality.

THE PROXIMITY TRAP

Among the many difficulties you face in organizational listening is the almost unavoidable tendency to listen more to those who have the most access to you.

Whether it's because you like them, or simply because they sit nearby, you converse with some people more than others.

This can lead to minor distortions, or it can cripple your ability to make decisions based on an accurate understanding of What's Going On Out There. In particular, in many organizations access and knowledge are inversely related: People in the field know what's really going on, but they have the hardest time reaching you.

Why do you think decisions that come from headquarters are so dopey so often?

---

[20] Worse. you're ignorant. And worse than that, you're intentionally ignorant.

Consultative decision-making involves a straight-line connection between information gathering and a single decision. The more general art of listening does the same thing, only in a many-to-many fashion.

Think of it this way: You make decisions all the time. It makes no sense to embark on a separate information-gathering expedition for every single one. So reserve formal, directed information-gathering for the formal decisions discussed in Chapter Three. For the day-to-day decisions that are a part of the ongoing life of any manager, if you're constantly in listening mode your decisions will be consultative. Just as important, those who report to you will understand that they're consultative because they'll have experienced you listening to them on a regular basis.

Listen. Listen to your employees, your peers, those to whom you report, experts and pundits (but skeptically – most of them have an axe to grind and sadly, too few have scruples about distorting the facts), and of course, high-integrity authors[21].

Understand not only the facts of the situation, but also your biases, which you use to filter the facts as you interpret them. If you don't, you won't make smart decisions.

How should you go about listening? This isn't a facetious question, or even one easily answered. When you're a line supervisor with a staff of ten, it isn't too difficult. You can talk to everyone directly. But what do you do with a staff of a hundred or more employees and several layers of management between most of them and you?

That's where it gets interesting. You have a variety of listening tools at your disposal when you lead a large organization. That's the good news. The bad news is, each of

[21] He said with appropriate humility.

them has significant limitations. Table 8.1 shows why.

When you're gathering information ... when you're listening ... you're trading off several different factors:

▶ The importance of using time efficiently.

▶ Your need for objective, fact-based data.

▶ The hazards associated with information that's biased and filtered[22].

▶ Recognition that nothing is as simple as it seems – that there are nuances of meaning difficult to recognize when you're looking at a situation from the outside.

▶ An obligation to get early warnings about major issues before they become major problems[23].

Here's your challenge: Not one of the listening channels

TABLE 8.1/ *LISTENING TOOLS*

Listening tool	Uses time efficiently	Objective	Unfiltered	Provides nuances	Reveals major issues
Metrics	X	X	X		X
Chain of command	X				
Walking around			X	X	
Open door policy			X	X	X
Suggestion box	X		X		X
Employee surveys	X	X	X		X
Employee round tables			X	X	X
Anonymous mailbox	X		X		X

[22] Which is to say, some people tell you what makes them look good rather than what you need to know.

[23] Yes, problems. "Problem" is a forbidden word in business, where political correctness is a force stronger by far than you'd find anywhere else. Ever since Dorye Roettger said, "There are no problems – only opportunities to be creative," usually truncated so the last three words are lost (and preceded by the industrialist John Henry Kaiser, who said, "Problems are only opportunities in work clothes,") it's been *de rigueur* for factory foremen ... uh, forepeople ... to say, after bursting into an executive council meeting, "We have a terrific opportunity – our factory just exploded."

available to you serves all of these purposes, and the one most leaders rely on the most – the chain of command – is the worst of the bunch by all measures except for the efficient use of time[24]. What can you do about these limitations? Very little. For the most part these properties are intrinsic to the channels.

You can improve the reliability of your chain of command somewhat, by hiring and promoting the right people and providing both leadership training and the right example. Even with all of that, in an organization of any size there are going to be managers who don't recognize issues, conceal them, or spin, consciously or unconsciously, what they report up the chain.

But wait – it gets worse. One bad manager has a hard time hiding in a good organization. If only one is bad, you'll find out from his or her manager, but if two are bad they'll each find ways to shield the other. And since in general, bad managers hire bad subordinates ... like hires like, you'll recall ... in very short order it's easy for whole branches of the chain of command to become completely unreliable sources of information. Since these are the very managers you most need to find and deal with, the whole situation can get entirely out of hand.

While the chain of command is the worst of your listening channels, the others are far from perfect. Your only recourse is to use them all, hoping each will compensate for the limitations of the others.

Which leaves just one remaining dilemma: how much time to invest in listening activities. The answer to that is, "a lot."

---

[24] Think of King Harry in Shakespeare's *Henry V* before the battle of Agincourt – he didn't rely on his chain of command to find out what his troops were thinking. He disguised himself and wandered among them, mostly listening to what they were talking about. What – you thought Ken Blanchard invented management by walking around?

So the last piece of the listening puzzle is to establish a time budget. Decide in advance how much time you plan to spend alleviating the isolation and consequent ignorance that's the natural condition of every leader.

There's one other vitally important reason for you to listen: So that when you talk, you can do so effectively. But this aspect of listening is better discussed in the contexts of presenting information effectively, and persuading.

PRESENTING INFORMATION

When most people hear the word "communicate" they think about presenting information. As a leader, when you think about presenting information, take a minute to ask yourself if that's really your goal.

Often, people present information because they've unconsciously decided to not provide leadership. "My job is to provide information," according to this way of thinking. "It's up to the listener to draw the right conclusion."

If this is how you think about the division of responsibilities, you aren't thinking like a leader. Leaders get others to follow … they persuade.

There are times leaders do need to present information without any attempt to persuade. Most often, these happen in the context of tasks, goals or ongoing responsibilities that have been delegated to lower levels of the organization. When you've delegated responsibility, one of the responsibilities you haven't delegated is providing the information necessary for success. This information could be related to tasks or job responsibilities, or it could be about the larger context within which the specific responsibility delegated is performed, recent events affecting the responsibility or employee, industry trends, or even the accomplishments of a team reporting to you that exemplifies a cultural trait you want to promote.

Which leads to the question of how to communicate effectively. The starting point is the *umwelt.*

COMMUNICATE WITHIN YOUR AUDIENCE'S *UMWELT*

What's an *umwelt?* *Umwelt* is a century-old concept introduced to ethology, the study of animal behavior, by Jakob von Uexküll. It's the recognition that every animal exists in a unique perceptual universe that's closed to human beings other than through inference: Much of a bee's world is ultraviolet; a dog's nose does a lot of what we use our eyes to accomplish. Then there are the electric fish[25] I studied in graduate school, which perceive their world through a sense we lack entirely.

Different people live in different *umwelts* too, although they aren't as hard to imagine as an olfactory universe, let alone an electric one. You've already gone through the trouble of trying to understand your audiences. Go one step further and try to see the world through their eyes and hear it through their ears. Then, you can find a way to present your message so it sounds like an extension of what each audience already knows and believes.

Or at least you can phrase your presentation based on their vocabulary and connect it to their experiences.

PRESENTING INFORMATION EFFECTIVELY

What are the steps to effective communication?

▶ *Understand your audience.* It's the *umwelt.* If you're

---

[25] Didn't I mention this? Electric fish are nifty little critters that produce electrical impulses roughly the same strength as a smoke detector battery and detect them through an array of sensory organs that cover their skin. They use these impulses to communicate with each other, and to detect objects in their environment. Try to imagine what that experience must be like and you'll gain some appreciation for the significance of the *umwelt* concept.

communicating with one executive, do everything you can to determine his or her "hot buttons": Key motivators, personal and organizational goals, likes and dislikes. If it's a small group, analyze each member this way. If it's a large group, divide it into categories and profile each category.

▸ *Determine your key messages.* You know way too much about this subject, and you're going to be tempted to explain everything you know. Resist the temptation. What you have to say is the center of your cosmos, but it's just one asteroid in your audience's solar system. Choose no more than five core messages (three is better). If you can't winnow your list down that far, you need to pull back to a higher-level perspective. (We'll revisit core messages in the context of persuasion – the idea is even more important there.)

▸ *Choose your medium.* Your key messages and knowledge about your audience's preferred communication styles should determine the medium. "They should read their e-mail," is about as useful as any other choice that substitutes how things should be for how they actually are. If your audience is an executive who wants to look you in the eye, make sure you meet face-to-face. And even though you "... like to scribble on the whiteboard while I'm talking," ... that's *your* preference. If your audience will reject your message because whiteboard-scrawling connotes lack of preparation, stuff your preference in the closet and prepare a formal PowerPoint presentation. Or vice versa.

▸ *Use formatting to reinforce your message:* When you communicate face-to-face, your vocal intonation and body language deliver as much information as your words. In memos and reports, intonation and body language aren't available to you. That's what formatting is for – to substitute for them. You know what your key messages are. How are you going to make sure the reader remembers them?

The act of formatting helps you think things through. Deciding what to bold or italicize, what to put in a bulleted or numbered list, what to separate into a sidebar, what to illustrate through a chart or graphic ... or in PowerPoint, whether and how to animate a graphic or bulleted list, and what to put into a "kicker box" at the bottom ... these decisions help you think through your message.

Carefully chosen formatting can have another benefit: It constitutes "meta-communication" – communication about the communication. It says you've thought through your communication instead of just blurting everything out. That's a good message to send.

Some leaders dispense information sparingly, limiting it to a "need to know." I agree, with this caveat: Your goal is followership, which means what they need to know is everything that can help them make smarter decisions on your behalf.

PERSUASION

That you need to persuade in order to lead barely needs mention. How to persuade is a very different question. Persuasion starts with listening and requires all the techniques of presenting information effectively. That, however, is just background. Persuasion takes these to the next level – the level of leadership.

As Chapter One pointed out, the starting point for leadership is envisioning the future – defining what you want to achieve, and making sure you're confident it's a good idea. If you don't know what you want to accomplish and understand the logic behind it … clearly and precisely … you're going to have a hard time persuading anyone else it's a good idea.

Just because it's a good idea from where you sit doesn't make it a good idea from where anyone else sits, of course. If it did, persuasion would be easy. For example: Imagine your business goal is to reduce the average cost of systems maintenance by contracting with an offshore-based systems integrator for legacy systems maintenance while making as much use as possible of application service providers (ASPs) for non-legacy applications. From your perspective as CIO it's a very good idea. You can be quite sure your IT staff won't share your view, even though it's for the good of the company. It isn't, after all, in their best interests, and capitalism isn't supposed to be a bastion of altruism.

Since you aren't dealing with stupid people, you need to establish a realistic target – what, that is, you're going to try to persuade the IT staff to do.

Here's the process:
▶ *Define your business goal and core messages.*
▶ *Understand your audiences.*
▶ *Define your goal for each audience.*
▶ *Connect their goals to your goals.*

DEFINE YOUR BUSINESS GOAL AND CORE MESSAGES

If you don't know what you're trying to accomplish, persuading others to help you accomplish it is going to be mighty difficult. If this point isn't clear, re-read Chapter One.

Now that you know, don't explain it. Presenting everything

you know is a thoroughly ineffective approach to persuasion that's popular, especially among technical professionals accustomed to understanding subjects in depth.

Contrary to popular belief, this usually isn't the result of a presenter who loves to show off. The motivation is far more noble than that. Experts in any subject love their subject – that's why they became an expert in it. And when you love a subject you want your audience to love it, too.

So the first step in simplifying your message is reminding yourself that your audience doesn't love the subject the way you do. Far from it: They find it complicated, difficult to understand, and probably tedious as well.

The antidote to this very common audience reaction is to prefer clarity to completeness.

Simplify your explanation it to its essence. The cliché, which regrettably is hard to improve on, is to develop your "elevator speech," which is to say, imagine you and someone important to achieving the goal find yourselves on an elevator. How do you explain what you're trying to achieve before one of you gets off the elevator?

The best formula to help you craft your elevator speech comes from journalism: Develop crisp, bulleted answers to six questions: Who, what, when, where, why, and how. Remember – crisp, bulleted answers, not long, rambling narratives. Your goal is to persuade, not to bore.

But change the order. Best is probably what, why, how, when, where, and who. But not always. To decide on the best order of presentation (among other issues) you need to consider who you're talking to.

UNDERSTAND YOUR AUDIENCES

Before you're allowed to persuade someone to follow you, you first need to understand them. That's because everyone in the world looks at the world through their own eyes, and with the exception of true altruists[26] they make decisions based on what they perceive to be their own best interests.

Some leaders are under the mistaken assumption that "best interests" means the same thing for everyone – generally, whatever it is that motivates the leader; usually money. That isn't the case. Different people are motivated by different things. Not uniquely different, of course, but different.

In the context of business change, the list of different audience goals is actually quite short. Start with the standard motivators (Chapter Five): Fear and the need to avoid it, greed, need for approval, and exclusivity. Add these, the most common drivers of resistance to business change: Need for job security, desire for career advancement and personal achievement, and preference for mental laziness.

The final item, mental laziness, calls for a few words of explanation. Few employees have an aversion to hard work. Most, though, jealously guard hard-won skills that might be invalidated, in part because those skills make them part of an elite group (exclusivity) but also because if those are invalidated they'll have to learn new ones. Even among IT professionals, this trait is sadly well-developed. Most people dislike learning and avoid having to think very hard – one reason "trusting your gut instincts" is such a popular decision-making technique despite its poor track record.

To define realistic goals for what you try to persuade each audience to do, you need to understand what's driving them. So listen to them, through all the channels described in the section on listening. In particular, listen for signs of the above-mentioned drivers of resistance.

[26] A species that's the object of an intense search by cryptobiologists when they aren't otherwise occupied by trying to find the yeti, bigfoot, and Loch Ness monster.

And do one more thing: Interpret. What people say isn't always what they mean, and in particular their objections to a business change rarely match what they're thinking and feeling. That's because, in our culture at least, employees are taught that loyalty to their employer is a virtue and self-interest is not. So they're likely to rationalize, which is to say they're going to find reasons your goals are either stupid or unethical. They are, that is, in search of ammunition.

DEFINE YOUR GOAL FOR EACH AUDIENCE

"Our goal isn't to get employees to like this change," read a communication plan produced by a depressingly high-priced management consulting firm. "It's to get them to understand."

In the course of your career you'll find yourself leading any number of changes employees won't like, not because employees automatically resist change but because some changes the organization needs to implement won't be good for all employees.

Does that mean you should give up? Of course not. You have many more choices than "get them to like" and "get them to understand."

When you're leading change, which is to say when you're leading, aim higher than that. Until it's demonstrated to be impossible, your goal should always be commitment to the change. That means employees need to understand the necessity, see a path to personal benefit, and believe the company will support, encourage and reward those who support the change, commit to its success, and help drive it to completion.

This goal won't always fit all audiences. When the business change will lead to layoffs for some employees and career disappointments for others, for example, trying to persuade those on the wrong end of the equation to commit to the change isn't just unrealistic, it's cruel.

Establish different goals for these audiences, by all means, but still, set your sights higher than "understand," even if it's nothing more than "passively acquiesce without resisting."

CONNECT THEIR GOALS TO YOUR GOALS

When you talk, you're providing information, ideas, and logic. Most people make up their minds first and then look for ammunition, selectively accepting only what supports their pre-existing biases. Put these two facts together and you're left with an unavoidable conclusion: Most people won't listen to you on any subject that matters to them unless you're feeding them ammunition.

Many otherwise talented communicators consider this to be an insurmountable barrier. Completely unethical propagandists consider the same reality to be their greatest asset. You? You don't have to abandon your integrity to persuade people to follow your lead.

What you do have to do is connect your goals to their goals. You need them to consider your arguments to be ammunition for their biases, and following you to be the best way to achieve their goals, whether those goals are avoidance of fear, desire for job security, a strong preference for mental laziness, or what have you.

Example: The company has decided to implement a comprehensive ERP suite, retiring a number of legacy systems as part of the program. This will require extensive retraining on the part of many business employees who spent years becoming proficient in multiple mainframe systems. It will also require extensive retraining on the part of many IT staff members who have extensive expertise in VSAM, CICS, and COBOL, since the ERP suite is built on a relational database and object-oriented programming tools, and ships with a proprietary scripting language used for most customization.

And one more thing: Right now, the company's information technology is used for record-keeping after the work is done. The plan is for the ERP suite to drive work through the company.

How do you connect business goals to audience goals?

Use the IT employees as an example. They've spent years acquiring skills that are about to become irrelevant. They're going to be feeling insecure about their jobs. At the same time they're about to face a difficult transition – they're accustomed to being experts, and are about to become novices. How do you connect your goals to their goals?

First, establish what it's going to take to achieve job security. What's that? You're going to fire them all and bring in a new team that knows the ERP suite? Shame on you. It's a bad strategy, demonstrating to all employees that they're fungible, only valuable until their particular skills aren't needed anymore. Think the good ones will stay? Think again – everyone who can leave will leave, and you'll be left running an organization of mediocrities and worse.

Re-read Chapter Four (*Staffing*).

Now … what's it going to take to achieve job security? Commitment to learning the new application and commitment to helping the company achieve a smooth, successful transition. Not only that, but through the new system's implementation, IT's role in the enterprise will be redefined. Currently, IT is a service provider. By being more closely involved in the company's business processes, the implementation emphasizes the additional value employees provide the company when compared to outside contractors.

Doesn't that conflict with the desire for mental laziness? In part. The solution to this is to emphasize the importance of the knowledge and skills you're still going to need –

understanding of the business, how to analyze business needs and develop efficient IT solutions and so forth – placing more focus on continuity.

Along with this emphasis on continuity, be frank about the importance of continuous learning while expressing confidence in the ability of a talented staff to acquire new skills.

A FEW FINAL THOUGHTS ABOUT PERSUASION

ESTABLISH TRUST

Persuasion requires more than just technique. Before you can persuade anyone, they first have to trust you. They don't have to like you, although it helps, but they do have to trust you, for the simple and obvious reason that you can't persuade anyone who doesn't believe what you say.

How do you go about establishing trust? The simplest and easiest way is to make a habit of telling the truth.

As if you needed a book to tell you that.

The advantages of telling the truth are pretty obvious – you don't get caught in a lie, your messages are automatically consistent, and most people consider telling the truth to be the hallmark of a trustworthy human being.

There are, of course, a few disadvantages as well[27]: If you aren't very careful, telling the truth will turn out to be incompatible with many of the other requirements for successful persuasion. Especially, telling the truth can mean offending your audience, complicating your message, and arguing.

Resorting to falsehoods certainly isn't the answer, of

[27] Right around here, many people become self-righteous about their integrity, forgetting that social conventions take precedence over brutal honesty. Or, as Jim Carrey pointed out in *Liar, Liar*, no matter what their wives actually look like when pregnant, husbands have only one acceptable response when asked, "Do I look fat?"

course – once you're caught in a lie, you've established yourself as someone who presents falsehoods and facts with equal facility and you'll be met with disbelief for a long time to come. There's a second well-known disadvantage to lying: It's hard to keep track and eventually you contradict yourself.

The resolution to this conundrum is to find that fine line that allows you to say anything you need to say to any audience you need to say it to: Perfecting the art of diplomatic phrasing.

Or as a manager once advised me after a particularly disastrous meeting, "Bob, you can say anything you want, but you can't say it any way you want."

The fine art of diplomacy is, sadly beyond the reach of this book. If you find yourself offending everyone you talk to, you need an executive coach, or perhaps different parents. If all you need is a pointer or two, here are two:

USE REPETITION TO YOUR ADVANTAGE

Just because you explained something once, that doesn't mean your audience understood you as you intended, accepted your message if they did, or even remember it now.

And you aren't just presenting information – you're trying to persuade. From the perspective of your audience that means getting comfortable with a new idea or way of thinking, figuring out whether it's advantageous to support it, and perhaps to start understanding your *umwelt*. Just saying it once gets it off your chest. It's unlikely to persuade.

Marketers divide markets into pioneers, early adopters, the middle market, late adopters, and hold-outs. You're marketing a new way of doing things and your audience will fall into the same categories.

The pioneers got there before you did. Saying it once is more than you need to persuade them. All you've done is

COMMUNICATION

inform them that you've caught up to where they already
were.

Early adopters get it with one or two hearings. They're
primed and ready for new ideas. No problems there.

Your middle market, which is to say most of the people
you need to persuade, are the ones who need most of your
repetitions. They need to be confident you're serious; they
need reassurance that this really is to their benefit or can be;
and they need to be sure they understand it properly. You
need to do more than just say it over and over to these folks.
You need to say it in different ways, so your message
connects to the different *umwelts* that exist in what you think
of as one undifferentiated group.

How about late adopters? Don't wait for them. Persuade
the middle market and rely on the middle market to persuade
the late adopters.

As for the hold-outs, they aren't going to make it. Not
everyone succeeds in any change. Your responsibility is to
create an environment in which everyone can succeed and
understands the rules for success. You can't succeed on their
behalf.

DON'T ARGUE

Arguing is pointless. It's like trying to persuade using
nothing but facts and logic, only worse. You can't win by
arguing, specifically because arguing has winners and losers.
Unless you think the person you're arguing with will enjoy the
experience of losing to you in a battle of wits, consider this: If
you lose the argument, you lose the argument; if you win the
argument the other person will just wait until you leave to
figure out why you're wrong, and you still won't win.

Arguments are about winning and losing. Discussions are
about mutual problem-solving. Whenever you find yourself in

an argument, find a way to turn it into a discussion as quickly as possible. It usually takes little more than asking, "What problem are we trying to solve?" If it does take more, follow that with, "Is there a way to blend our approaches? I really like this about yours …"

ONE-ON-ONE COMMUNICATION

One-on-one communication includes such minor matters as coaching, feedback, and giving bad news. There's less difference between this and group communication than you might think. Whether your task is to persuade a group to embrace the direction you're setting for the organization or an individual to shape up as an alternative to shipping out, the rules are the same.

The biggest difference between one-on-one communication and group communication is that the former requires more courage, for at least two reasons.

The first is that it requires you to look an individual in the eye and say things the other person might not want to hear. This is harder for some than for others; few find it easy. But it's a critical element of leadership: If an employee's work is substandard and you don't let him or her know, you're doing neither of you a favor.

It hurts you because you'll continue to get substandard work until you do intervene. You're doing the employee a disservice as well. You're in a situation with only two possibilities –the employee either is or is not capable of better work. If it's the former, your failure to intervene holds the employee back. If it's the latter, the employee is better off knowing that this situation isn't going to work out. An early warning is far kinder than an abrupt termination sometime in the future.

The second reason direct communication requires courage

is that it's open to immediate challenge, As a leader you can't wait for certainty before you act in many situations, including the times you have to respond to "coaching opportunities." Nor is incomplete information the only avenue for challenges. Some of what you have to communicate will inevitably be subjective, open to debate simply because it's about something, such as aesthetics or ethics, that can't be resolved through the use of facts and logic.

You have to communicate anyway, despite your lack of certainty. When challenged you need the courage to hold your ground when necessary; to agree to re-think your conclusions when appropriate, and, at times, to agree that there's no one right answer, and in the absence of objective truth the employee has to abide by your judgment while in your organization.

FINAL THOUGHT

There's a lot to think about when you have to communicate, whether it's to listen, to inform, or to persuade. So much so that it's easy to get lost in technique and forget the point of it all.

So here's a shortcut to use when all else fails. It's the single most important element of any effective communication.

It's empathy. Empathize with your audience and it's hard to go wrong. After you've planned the communication and before you execute, ask yourself this:

How would I respond if I were on the other side of the transaction?

Ask yourself this, give yourself an honest answer, and you'll do fine.

SUMMARY

▶ Communication is the core skill that allows leaders to

accomplish all of the others. It consists of three very different activities: listening, presenting information, and persuasion.

▶ Listening is how leaders avoid ignorance. Unfortunately, every listening channel available for leadership use is flawed. The only solution is to use them all. Which is why leaders have to budget time for organizational listening.

▶ Leaders present information effectively to enable *followership* – the ability of those they lead to lead on their behalf. Followership requires specific information, and it requires context so managers and staff can make decisions intelligently. The following steps provide a framework for presenting information effectively:
  ▷ Understand your audience.
  ▷ Determine your key messages.
  ▷ Choose your medium.
  ▷ Use formatting to reinforce your message.

▶ Persuasion is the essence of leadership – by definition it's how you get others to follow. The framework for persuasion is similar to the framework for presenting information:
  ▷ Define your business goal and core messages.
  ▷ Understand your audiences.
  ▷ Define your goal for each audience.
  ▷ Connect their goals to your goals.

▶ Persuasion requires more than following a framework. In particular, remember the importance of establishing trust; use repetition to your advantage; and above all, don't argue.

Final thoughts

I recently watched one of the extra features of the second
Lord of the Rings DVDs – the one explaining how director
Peter Jackson and company devised the astonishing
Smeagol/Gollum character. While the story has its share of
technological wizardry, the amazing technology isn't at the
heart of this story, even though Smeagol, the most complex
and interesting character in the film, is computer-generated.

The story of how Smeagol came to life is a story of
exemplary leadership, the more so because not one of the
dozen or more people who described the process even
mentioned Peter Jackson's leadership as a factor.

What's striking, when listening to their account of the
process, is the deep commitment everyone involved in the
project had to creating a phenomenal film; their mutual
respect and trust (and the long process they went through to
achieve it); and their willingness to put aside elements of their
original vision as they began to accept the contributions of
Andy Serkis, who they thought they'd hired to be nothing
more than "voice talent" but who entirely redefined the part.

It's an outstanding example of leadership at its finest.
Peter Jackson was able to enlist his entire production

company in his vision, establishing followership throughout. The team responsible for Smeagol, which included technical animators, artists, the aforementioned Andy Serkis, and the actors Elija Wood and Sean Astin (Frodo and Sam), all expressed a sincere, convincing focus on creating something remarkable, not on their need for screen time or recognition.

That's the essence of good leadership: Focusing a team on the goal. When a leader is able to do this, the result is magical ... literally so in the case of *Lord of the Rings* but no less so in a business organization.

This book is about how to lead IT effectively, and to a certain extent how to lead any organization effectively. There's a big difference, though, between leading effectively and leading well. As with many felonies, the difference is defined by your intentions.

Leading effectively means getting others to follow. Leading well means choosing good destinations, being honest in your communication, and otherwise choosing behaviors that pass ethical muster.

If you use the techniques described in this book, chances are good you'll become a more effective leader. Whether it will make you a better leader is beyond what this book has to offer, and probably beyond what any book about leadership can offer. Books can offer ideas; leaders have to choose their own paths or they're following rather than leading.

For whatever it's worth, here's an opinion: Excellent leaders are those who choose the organization they lead carefully, and then place the organization's goals ahead of their own. Choose the organization you lead carefully, because every organization exists for a purpose, and you have to embrace that purpose in order to provide leadership. If you're leading a philanthropic organization this is easier; philanthropic organizations exist to do good work, after all.

Some businesses only exist to make money or to "create shareholder value," sad to say. I don't personally think any of them will persist, because given a choice between buying from this kind of organization and others more focused on providing great products and services and taking excellent care of their customers, those whose first purpose is profit will inevitably lose ground.

But as a leader you might find yourself asked to take on a leadership role in an organization whose only real goal is profit, with everything else viewed as less-important means to this all-important end. My advice is to think carefully. The eight tasks of leadership presented in this book are difficult enough in an organization whose goals are intrinsically inspiring to employees. They're infinitely harder when the only purpose is to create shareholder value.

It's your choice, based on your values and goals. Being an effective leader is easier when your goals, the organization's goals, and the goals you establish for those you lead line up, but they don't have to. That's up to you – many leaders have private goals that are vastly different from those they espouse publicly. The techniques described in this book are useful either way.

It's up to you whether you use your newfound powers for good.